To

All my bosses and mentors who made a difference in my professional career.

"Resilient leadership necessitates a high level of self-awareness on the part of the leaders, as well as an understanding of how their verbal and non-verbal communication affects the team. Making errors is a natural part of the process. Nobody can accomplish everything perfectly the first time. Accepting mistakes, learning from them, and making course changes are all part of resilient learning."

- Dr. Amit Das, Motivational Speaker, Leadership Coach , Counsellor, and Mentor.

Contents

Foreword

Dear Reader,

Thank you for taking the time to learn more about resilient leadership and it's capabilities. This book,**"The Alchemy Of Resilient Leadership,"** aims to teach you how critical it is to be resilient every day toward achieving the things that matter most to you. Leaving no stone unturned, and to develop a mindset of seeing the most overlooked aspects of life not only for what they are or appear to be, but also for what they could be. The COVID-19 pandemic highlighted the importance of increasing societal resilience at multiple levels (nations, businesses, and individuals). In this business environment, which the book refers to as the "New Normal World," organisations navigate through a reset turbulence phase that is anticipated to continue for another few years. The book argues for the necessity for organisations to "reset for resilience" in order to face impending change (survive) and take advantage of the possibilities (thrive) presented by that transformation.

The author of **"The Alchemy Of Resilient Leadership"** explores many notions of flexible or resilient leadership, as well as why such leadership is necessary in today's organisations. This book,**"The Alchemy Of Resilient Leadership,"** is a quest to perceive even the most mundane things in a new light. Its goal is to assist you to harness your capacity to become more resilient and use it to your advantage in order to rise above the mediocre tides in all aspects of your life.

The characteristics of a resilient organisation are presented in depth in the book. The book also provides guidelines that leadership teams may evaluate and discuss as they decide whether to start their transformations into resilient businesses. The concept that resilience is a journey worth taking and not a black-or-white choice is conveyed throughout the book. The degree to which the management team may influence or control the acceptance of the book's concepts depends on the industry, strategic groupings, and geographical areas in which the organisation competes, as well as its strategy. As a result, management may establish a goal level of resilience that is appropriate for the strategic scenarios the organisation has chosen and can modify that objective as needed.

The importance of building resilient leaders, consumers, communities, the environment, and other stakeholders is also discussed in the book. The author make a plea to business leaders and outline a number of things they can do to build resilience, both within their own organisations and in the environments in which they operate. They truly hope that we, as a society, with all of its actors, will not waste this catastrophe. The experience of the COVID-19 pandemic and its ramifications has generated and will continue to generate enough impetus for contemplation, insights, and, most crucially, action, as expressed in the book.

The author recognises that intelligent, motivated individuals like you have special gifts to give the world, but it's difficult to do in this VUCCAD (Volatile, Uncertainty, complexity, conflicting, ambiguity, and dynamic) business environment. The author has been assisting managers in increasing their productivity, which he describes as the capacity to make progress on the results that matter most to them professionally and individually. This book, "**The Alchemy Of Resilient Leadership,**" aims to teach you how critical it is to be resilient every day toward achieving the things that matter most to you, leaving no stone unturned, and to develop a mindset of seeing the most overlooked aspects of life not only for what they are or appear to be, but also for what they could be. Through his profession, he's seen that the vast majority of time management advice offered doesn't help you enhance your life. Resilient leadership has been defined as a critical leadership method for dealing with resilient, rather than technical or predictable, difficulties, which are particularly common in complex situations. The book supports a new social contract, a rejuvenation of your civic life at a time when you most need it.

The author of this bookexplores many notions of adaptable and resilient leadership, as well as why such leadership is necessary in today's enterprises. Then numerous study streams that give helpful knowledge regarding flexible and resilient leadership are briefly presented. Although a complete and exhaustive examination was not possible, the author summarises his main findings and offers some practical advice for leaders on how to become more flexible and resilient in this VUCCAD corporate environment.

The only thing that stays the same in today's corporate climate is change, and change is more plentiful, quick, and complex than ever before. Change and upheaval are the new normal in today's corporate world. Organisations, and even entire sectors, can be turned completely upside down in an instant. Resiliency is no longer just a desirable trait in a leader; it's a necessity. Resilient leaders understand that leading and managing change is a need in today's business world, and they are constantly looking for new methods to solve new problems, learn new skills, and take on new challenges with a sense of grounded inventiveness.

This book outlines the importance of resilient leadership, clearing your head of clutter, and sticking to a single-point agenda. The days of traditional, stability-oriented organisations are numbered. Organisations built for both stability and dynamism with networks of teams and people-centered cultures governed by common goals and co-created value for all stakeholders are replacing them. The Business Dictionary defines " Resilient Leadership" as a "Chameleon-Like Personality" capable of keeping up with fast changes in its environment.

During these times of upheaval and uncertainty, many companies recognise the need for speed. Leaders perceive an opportunity to accelerate their organisations' pace by doing even more in the areas mentioned above in the future. Respondents most typically cite more efficient decision making, clearer communication, and the use of technology to better engage consumers and employees when asked about the key chances to attain higher speed. The author offers the most effective tactics and step-by-step instructions for you to construct your own particular road to excellence in this book. You'll also find better methods to collaborate with colleagues, respond more effectively to coaching and mentoring, and become more positive and self-directed in your thoughts and actions, resulting in more personal and professional pleasure. This book attempts to provide insights into the many pathways, courses, and drives that world-class enterprises have constructed in order to achieve the pinnacles of greatness. This book provides cutting-edge material, including innovative and unusual study aids as well as fresh, thought-provoking content, with an emphasis on integrating corporate agility, or resilientness, into practical management.

Regardless of the audience or venue, reading this book puts the reader on a unique and advantageous platform to connect in a more intelligent and successful manner. This book is well-researched and educational for people of all ages and genders. This book is a quest to perceive even the most mundane things in a new light. Its goal is to assist you to harness your capacity to become more resilient and use it to your advantage in order to rise above the mediocre tides in all aspects of your life. It reveals numerous methods for intentionally cultivating a mindset that refuses to be superficial about life.

To survive and prosper, a leader must be able to foresee, plan for, respond to, and adapt to problems and opportunities. It goes beyond risk management to take a more comprehensive view of an individual's health and performance. A "Resilient Leadership" is one that not only survives, but also flourishes in the long run, surviving the test of time. Techniques work well for the simple and the complicated, but not so well for the complex. The complex requires a new strategy, with the goal of making the organisation being led more nimble and self-organising. Dr. Amit Das has designed a straightforward and step-by-step method for Leadership based on his work, complex resilient leadership, while challenging and questioning the reader to be more successful and less busy. This book will appeal to practitioners who want to increase their leadership effectiveness. It is an essential tool for the time-pressed leader and manager. It will also be of interest to leadership students and academics.

Every organisation relies on its leadership to strengthen, organise, and shift resources in order to make the most efficient and effective use of them in order to enhance returns on investment and develop resilientness.

Dr. Amit Das provides a step-by-step approach in this book on how to create an excellent resilient culture at your organisation. The author demonstrates how to uncover your hidden culture, transform ideals into actions, and open up communication across layers. To keep your culture thriving for the long term, the author emphasises the significance of being clear from the top, building trust, and providing support structures. As Dr. Amit Das demonstrates in his book, by building your culture, you can increase communication, raise morale, encourage trust, and keep negativity at bay within your team.

The author provides businesses with a step-by-step strategy for analysing, creating, and implementing iterative resilient cultural transformation, with each success building on prior achievements. As a result, the organisation continues to adapt in ways that reduce stress, encourage learning, and promote organisational wellness. Indeed, it may have increased as businesses realise their present systems are incapable of keeping up with the current rate of change. Transformation is not without danger, but adopting agility may mitigate this by giving organisations the resilience they need to deal with constant change. Consider whether your processes are flexible enough. Could your essential business systems adapt quickly to significant operational changes?

The book draws on first-hand experience from high-performance operations to deliver vital resilient leadership lessons as well as clear, accessible, and practical insights on managing teams in any corporate setting. This book provides a new and fascinating viewpoint on the factors that influence team and organisational greatness. Dr. Amit Das, the book's author, has a unique combination of expertise and insight, having worked as a management consultant. His insights and interviews from business sectors are used to demonstrate the obstacles to high performance and leadership.

The materials include a performance model that can be applied to a wide range of organisations, focusing on people's attitudes rather than skills; a process for closing the gap between desired and actual outcomes; how to accelerate performance in real time; exhibiting a set of behaviours that the capacity of an organisation to function efficiently, adapt properly, adjust correctly, and grow from within is referred to as organisational health. The author also looks at whether great leaders are born or made, how lean ideas are used differently in various organisations, and why clever individuals fail so often after being promoted to management positions. Take a path that leads to significant performance increases and a great culture where everyone is prepared to succeed with this leadership. Just like strategy, writing a book takes deep contemplation to narrate a theory in a very lucid manner. Hence, the author could establish his thought process for readers.

Once again, thank you for taking the time to learn more about resilient leadership capabilities. Thank you for taking the time to read this book.

So, happy reading and learning to all my readers.

Carpe diem.

Dr. Amit Das

Leadership Coach , Counsellor, and Mentor.

Preface

"In order to achieve organisational goals, being resilient is preferable to being process-focused."

Excellent leaders are flexible. The capacity to pivot in response to new or possible challenges and opportunities is what makes someone adaptable; it goes beyond simply changing one's appearance or place of employment. Leaders that are flexible see the distinction between technical and flexible difficulties. In ways never seen before, the COVID-19 pandemic had increased the pace of disruption and exposed the degree of globalisation and the interconnectedness of technology, business, and society. This transition had also exposed the volatility of individuals formerly regarded as industry leaders.

In the corporate world, transformative changes happen quickly, so it's important to keep on top of them with creativity and openness. With this book find out more about the resilient leadership style and how it may help you lead your organisation through problems of this nature.

Leadership must be resilient in the face of VUCCAD (Volatile, Uncertain, Complex, Conflicting, Ambiguous, and Dynamic) business landscape.

What if you were told to put this knowledge to use by creating a leadership style that was noticeably different and superior to others? These are the options presented in the book Resilient Leadership's deceptively straightforward tale. The leadership approach they provide fulfils my promise of a new way of seeing, thinking, and leading in addition to other things. Executives who are trying to succeed in a setting of rising volatility, uncertainty, complexity, conflicting, ambiguity, and dynamic face significant obstacles from intense demands. Leaders of today struggle continually to make sense of their shifting environments and decide what is best for themselves, their teams, and their businesses.

Every change comes with difficulties, and it is the leader's responsibility to meet them head-on. Understanding human needs and the repercussions of failing to fulfil them is essential for addressing change, conflict, and the roadblocks and sticking points that can prevent the best possible corporate performance.

Resilience, however, is not a given. It is a dynamic ability that can be developed and strengthened, and there are many different techniques on various levels to increase a manager's resilience. To help leaders understand how one links to the other and how each may be utilised to improve personal and collective resilience, I made a distinction between personal resilience, the "resilience field," and features of resilient leadership.

I have outlined specific, doable strategies for getting past impediments to resilience development at all levels, enhancing the capacity of the individual leader, teams, groups, and organisations to persevere in the face of adversity. To improve their ability to overcome challenges and adversity and to foster an atmosphere where employees inside a organisation may flourish and grow, leaders can use the doable actions and methods described in this book.

Corporate executives at all levels confront increasing hurdles in figuring out how to handle disruptive work conditions and unpredictability as the world changes and businesses increase in both size and complexity. Most executives are taught to concentrate on the rational system, which includes things like growth objectives, revenue and expense tracking, and strategic planning. The emotional system, an instinctive pattern of behaviours, responses, and interactions that shapes people, teams, and organisations, is something that is frequently disregarded but is still essential to successful leadership.

Resilient leaders are able to maintain composure, objectivity, and morality in the face of mounting stress and rapid change. You'll discover how to successfully navigate the predictable but sometimes unnoticed patterns that appear in every organisation's emotional system during times of uncertainty and transition in this insightful and cutting-edge guide. Each chapter includes three "big ideas" that present fresh ways of seeing, thinking, and leading, as well as recommended fundamental techniques for putting them into practice.

You'll learn how to maintain a calm and steady leadership presence in the face of everyday challenges, respond boldly to opposition and risk, build strong relationships with coemployees and direct reports, and recognise your own leadership strengths and shortcomings. To bring about change, you must first establish yourself as the authority that others want to follow.

Change may be frightening, disturbing, and disconcerting. Fear, tension, resentment, and resistance can arise even when change is anticipated or desired. These reactions to change are frequently perceived by leaders as a hurdle that must be overcome. Resilient leaders must be able to determine when to enter the conflict and when to exit and observe from the sidelines.

Change is unavoidable in today's enterprises. It means in business, change is the only constant, although it is rarely as unexpected or as overpowering as it has been in 2022. During their careers, the majority of these executives claim to have been through many acquisitions, mergers, reorganisations, or other significant organisational changes. They show that the rate and magnitude of change are both increasing. Recognising that change is unavoidable is not the same as effectively dealing with it. Many leaders have little or no awareness of or training in navigating the change process, despite the fact that their capacity to react to, manage, control, and promote change is critical to their success.

The coronavirus pandemic has upended a number of industries, from hospitality to energy, that appeared positioned for success in the new decade until lately. Businesses are now scrambling to pick up the debris while navigating an uncertain future. Under normal conditions, change management is a difficult task. Accepting change is the definition of resiliency. Resiliency is the practice of fine-tuning methods. While agility or resiliency has always been crucial in the modern workplace, it is now more important than ever. Situations that are volatile, uncertain, complex, and uncertain have never been harsher, and the need for resilient leadership has never been more critical.

- How can resilient leadership work in the real world?
- What is the best way to teach it through leadership development programs?
- Which tools help it improve its practice and teaching?
- What are the connections between adaptive leadership and other important ideas and practices?

This book answers these and other issues by demonstrating how resilient leadership methods are used to handle some of the world's most serious challenges—political and cultural divides, remote work, and crisis management—across a wide range of industries.

Traditional leadership patterns were beginning to fail even before the unprecedented difficulties of 2020. You saw an obvious need for it as companies advanced and expanded against a backdrop of continual social, technical, and cultural development, and you saw the need to move away from management methods that place a deterministic focus on a single leader.

Global pandemics, business restructurings, downsisings, increased globalisation, and market upheavals are just a few of the unexpected challenges that leaders and their organisations must negotiate. Another driver of transition is the rapid evolution of technology, which necessitates continual retraining for individuals and organisations due to rising rates of obsolescence and replacement. Additionally, the people that make up organisations, work groups, and teams change regularly. Gradual changes in the external environment can result in a new danger or opportunity for the organisation. New rivals, new technology, social and cultural changes, new legal or regulatory rules, changes in economic situations, and changes in consumer wants and preferences are just a few examples. Instead of just improving a current strategy or relying on a planned contingency plan, successful adaptation to such changes sometimes necessitates an imaginative new approach.

In today's complicated VUCCAD settings, striking a balance between chaos and rigorous structure is critical. It might be difficult to create and maintain the ideal environment. Culture, ownership, mentality, feedback, and long-term objectives are all important. The leader must be able to handle a variety of situations, particularly new, changing, and ambiguous ones. It is connected with mode four leaders who have the agility to function in any mode and, most crucially, perceive things from many perspectives. The capacity to think in a variety of ways is what gives such leaders their flexibility. If you know that changes are occurring in the competitive environment, you can quickly determine who will be most resistant to the adjustment in priorities required to manage the new scenario. This book is for management teams that want to improve their organisation's ability to adapt to and respond to environmental changes. The majority of leadership assumptions are founded on a deterministic worldview.

Leadership has evolved in the era of knowledge and information, and it has become more interested in finding ways to survive that allow them to keep up with the environment and the next digital age, which will put it on the cusp of leadership wisdom. To be effective, a leader must strike a balance between goals that require difficult compromises, such as reliability and efficiency, and the requirement for creative resiliency to new threats and possibilities. Competing ideals and tradeoffs can sometimes result in actions that are diametrically opposed (e.g., controlling vs. empowering). Another example of resilient leadership is a leader's ability to balance opposing ideals and contrary styles of conduct in a way that is acceptable for the occasion. Moving from one post to another in the same organisation or to a higher one in a different organisation is common in a management career. Different sorts of management jobs, as well as positions in another organisation with a diverse objective or culture, require different patterns of conduct for effective leadership. By recognising these crucial shifts, describing the inner tensions they cause, and giving advice for effective navigation, I have given a framework for dealing with and responding to them. This outside-in approach identifies the most important leadership issues that CEOs will encounter when they mobilise their businesses to successfully adapt to competitive and environmental change. According to me, strategy is leadership because environmental changes necessitate alterations in strategic goals, which result in a constant pattern of resistance.

One of the pillars of resiliency is the ability to remain hopeful while remaining realistic. Successful adapters see change as an opportunity rather than a danger. They believe they can maintain their effectiveness in the new context. Managers' confidence in their ability to be effective during times of transition appears to be boosted by optimism. It's arguable whether optimism can be taught, but the next time you're in a circumstance that requires change, try discovering something positive and building on it. Make a note of the opportunities given by the transition and share them with the rest of the organisation.

Resilient leadership, if it existed at all, was not a well-known notion during Abraham Lincoln's time. Nonetheless, Lincoln had certain resilient leadership qualities that are worth considering. His openness to tolerating variety was one of these traits. Lincoln is alleged to have appointed his enemies to the cabinet on purpose. He desired to engage their divergent viewpoints in order to guide the country to the greatest answers. He was always open to criticism and discussion as a leader. In addition, Lincoln was empathic and fast at forming ties with the people he led. He effectively had an open-door policy, allowing individuals to come to him and talk about their problems. His compassionate posture and attentive ears helped him acquire the respect of people around him.

Management and leadership are two separate beasts. Management is concerned with dealing with complexity, people, and tasks, whereas leadership is concerned with dealing with change and ensuring that the team works together to achieve common goals. The most effective leaders are able to adapt quickly to changing situations and utilise the appropriate strategy for each occasion. Poor leaders, on the other hand, fail to change appropriately in dynamic situations, resulting in chaos and confusion. What happens if you put pressure on a crystal glass? It usually becomes weaker over time and finally breaks. Crystal glasses, like many other items and living things, are delicate. What is the polar opposite of delicate? Strong, tenacious, and resilient come to mind. Being robust, resilient, and flexible, on the other hand, is not the polar opposite of being fragile.

Leaders that learn and adapt to problems in a VUCCAD business environment have a significant competitive edge. Leaders must adjust as well, frequently making significant changes because their roles might be procedural and rule-driven. I haveexplained enough on how to apply systems thinking to any framework in order to become more resilient and effective in a rapidly changing world. Anyone who runs an organisation or an organisational endeavor will tell you that things are changing quickly and that the difficulties you all face are becoming more complicated. Leaders must be resilient and sensitive to the fast-changing world in order to flourish in this VUCCAD environment. This begins with paying attention to critical input that will lead you to the result you aim to achieve via your organisational efforts. It is your responsibility as a systems leader to build an organisation that can adapt to the difficulties it confronts on a daily basis.

In this book I will discuss how you may become a leader who thoroughly knows how you think, allowing your team to tackle any problem, issue, or scenario and turn insight into unique ideas for real effect and change. Systems thinking entails attempting to comprehend the systems that surround you. To do more than just respond to circumstances as they occur. Instead, consider how the world truly works. In today's fast-changing competitive VUCCAD world, merely pursuing efficiency would not be enough. So I will show you a framework for establishing resilient organisations that are quick and agile in responding to market changes.

Leaders must also realise that organisational results are not something that can be generated directly, but rather indirectly, through instilling a set of simple norms that govern each group member's work. To develop system-level behavior, you must concentrate on the underlying rules that generate it. The issue is that CEOs, administrators, and other organisational leaders are always striving to get more out of their teams and organisations in order to improve both internal efficiency and outward influence. They want to work smarter and leave a bigger impression on the world faster. The issue is that humans do not act like a collection of gears. Their intentions are often mixed, and you're all aware that they may participate in more subtle types of resistance, which gears do not.

I have emphasised the need for continuous professional growth. To avoid extinction, my formula asserts that an organisation's rate of learning must be equal to or greater than the rate of change in the environment. Fortunately, learning possibilities abound in today's environment, and this richness should be embraced as well as utilised. Resilient leaders encourage learning by cultivating a culture that appreciates it and actively shares it. To sum up, whether you're an individual or an organisation, you need to be resilient to construct resilient organisations to ensure organisational excellence and effectiveness if you want to survive and prosper in the 21st century.

"Your theoretical knowledge will provide you some concepts and insights on resilience, while your practical knowledge will give you tried-and-true methods for developing resilience. Therefore, knowledge—both theoretical and practical—is crucial to enhancing your resilience. It is more of a practical experience that contributes to resilience building when you put into a percentage."

-Dr. Amit Das

Leadership Coach , Counsellor, and Mentor.

Acknowledgements

*At the outset, I will thank my family for supporting me throughout the journey of writing my book and encouraging me to live my dreams; my son has always been instrumental in giving his inspiration to complete the writing of this book. Despite the fact that I am listed as the author of this book,"***The Alchemy Of Resilient Leadership,***" would not have been published if I had depended entirely on my own talents. Creating this book required more than anything—it took a family of dedicated and caring people who were always prepared to lend a hand.*

Writing a book while working full-time is no simple task, so I'd want to express my gratitude to my amazing coworkers who act as cheerleaders in equal measure. Thank you, too, to my students and clients for your patience and unflinching support while I worked on this book!

Thank you to everyone who has listened to me argue for doing everything you can to make your life, including your work life, more progressive. I appreciate everyone's assistance throughout the process. This book would not have been possible without each of you having had an impact on my life in some manner.

Lastly, I would like to thank all the people with whom I have been associated. You gave me power. I would like to thank Notion Press for publishing my book. Finally, thank you all for gifting your time to read this book.

I'd want to convey my heartfelt appreciation to the almighty God for bestowing his blessings and being so gracious.

CHAPTER ONE

The Journey Of Resilient Leadership Building In The VUCCAD Business World

"Become the kind of leader that people would follow voluntarily; even if you had no title or position." —Brian Tracy

Resilience is necessary for living a successful life and organisation. Successful commercial leadership requires a winning combination of strength and strategy, which all excellent leaders must possess in order to rapidly recover from setbacks and maintain stability and steadiness. Of course, every corporate executive will err from time to time. Giving oneself the opportunity to develop, learn, and change after a setback or a mistake is the key.

Resilient leadership is all about supporting, experimenting with, and implementing change, whether it comes in the form of policy or attitudes. Many individuals may feel frightened when you push through substantial changes that force you to confront people's accustomed worlds. However, as a leader, you must figure out a way to make it work.

What it is and Why it matters in business?

Resilient leadership is all about finding a means to dissatisfy and disapoint people in order to mobilise them for the real work that has to be done. People will be scared of you if you are an resilient leader. As an authority figure, you are responsible for guaranteeing the entity's life by offering guidance, protection, and order. As a resilient leader, you must be willing to upset the status quo and encourage people to go to new and unfamiliar locations that are potentially dangerous, unsettling, and confusing. Most businesses have minimal resilient leadership behavior because adaptive leaders must risk speaking what has to be stated rather than what others desire to hear.

Neuroscience research has shown that the brain is very flexible or malleable. You may thus learn how to develop resilience because you are not fixed at birth. This will be simpler for some people than for others. The good news is that you have a better chance of developing resilient leadership qualities the more difficult scenarios you are exposed to. Your brain can help you with this since it is built to support your ability to learn, adapt, and grow. Its innate survival system includes this. Therefore, the potential for development and resilience increases as problems increase.

Is successful leadership dependent on resilient leadership?

Resilient leadership entails determining who and what groups will suffer losses, as well as the nature of those losses. There are usually two sorts of talk going on in an organisational setting: what individuals say out loud and what they are truly saying in their brains. The most crucial information in every conversation is almost never uttered aloud.

Being a leader who can successfully navigate through problems and lead people with bravery and conviction requires developing resilience. I discovered that managers, peers, and direct subordinates see leaders with high levels of resilience as being more effective. An organisation that is resilient not only survives but also flourishes in a changing and unpredictable environment.

"Resilience is not a final state of being, but rather a process of adaptation and growth within a dangerous environment, claims a comprehensive research on leadership and resilience."

Resilience is your reaction to stress and how quickly you return to normal once the stressor has passed. According to this concept, resilience and stress are intrinsically intertwined. Being resilient will be considerably more difficult for leaders who are always under stress. Building leadership resilience requires effective stress management.

Resilient leadership focuses on change that allows people, organisations, and society to grow or thrive. The most prevalent cause of failure is treating adaptive challenges as if they were technical issues. The majority of issues are a combination of technical and adaptive obstacles. In the corporate sector, for example, a merger will involve technical elements, but the adaptive parts pose a bigger risk since the newly merged enterprises will need to change their cultural norms, power structures, and value systems.

The Center for Creative Leadership defines resilience as our capacity to react nimbly to difficulties. It is what enables us to overcome obstacles, endure disappointments, and succeed after failure in life. It involves more than just overcoming adversity or being strong in the face of difficulty. Growth is a part of resilient leadership as well. This definition emphasises the significance of personal development. There must be change for progress to take place. Although change is often difficult, it is important. You must have the ability to adapt and welcome change if you want to develop resilient leadership qualities.

- How can you develop the capacity to maintain your enthusiasm under stress, to handle any disruptive changes, and to adapt?
- How can you recover quickly after failures or any setbacks?
- How can you conquer significant obstacles without acting dysfunctionally or hurting other people?

There is no exact formula for predicting the future of any industry; nonetheless, business executives can envision the next day based on the unique qualities of each organisation. Without resilient leaders, it is impossible to create resilient teams. Resilient businesses have strong cultures built on trust, accountability, and adaptability, as well as competent leadership at all levels. The capacity to bounce back rapidly from difficulty, adversity, or disaster is referred to as "resilience."

Professor Nancy Koehn of Harvard Business School asserts, "Resilience is the potential to not just tolerate big obstacles, but to become stronger in the middle of them," as more persuasive evidence. We live in a society that is filled with crisis after crisis—tragedy after calamity, emergency following unexpected, often challenging surprise—like waves breaking on the shore. Additionally, leaders have a significant impact on others around them due to their position. It is therefore much more important for leaders to be resilient and successful under stress. if the leader is killed. The group loses. You are the ship's captain as a leader. You and your team will arrive at your destination unharmed if you develop your resilient leadership talents.

Resiliency and constant innovation are essential for survival.

There are various paradigms and definitions of leadership agility. The paradigm of one distinctive leadership style is slipping away in current times, and each scenario will require a different sort of leader. The team's agility is becoming increasingly important. As a result, leadership agility is built on an agile team that can pivot in a new direction as the situation requires. Resilient leaders strike a compromise between their ideal vision of what they want to achieve and the realities of their lives and schedules.

In 2022, the top ten most innovative organisations in the workplace In the midst of an enormous upheaval in where and how they work, Miro, Carrot Fertility, Indeed, Dropbox, Dialpad, Atlassian, and Slack are all navigating the transformation with fresh services in the midst of an enormous upheaval in where and how they work. Explore the whole list of Fast Organisation's Most Innovative

Companies for 2022, which includes 528 companies that are redefining their sectors, businesses, and culture. They chose the most impactful organisations in 52 categories, including the most innovative enterprises, media, and personal finance enterprises.

"You can't build an resilient organisation without resilient people--and individuals change only when they have to, or when they want to." -Gary Hamel

A successful strategy in a digital environment necessitates critical decisions about which markets to pursue and what products or services are required to win. However, outer-game concerns should not eclipse the inner-game imperatives of developing a data-driven and resilient organisation model. After all, a flexible organisation ensures that businesses allocate the appropriate people and resources to their most critical opportunities. During the epidemic, one of the most important lessons learned was that every organisation must learn to anticipate and manage change and unpredictability. You've all heard it before: the speed of change has never been quicker, and it's not going to slow down anytime soon. And technology CEOs are frequently at the forefront of change.

Resilient leaders are always looking for new methods to match pivotal events with shifting consumer preferences. They are attempting to alter client preferences in ways that benefit both their companies and their customers. They train their employees for both expected and unexpected outcomes. They can feel when things are about to change and react rapidly. These resilient leaders do a great job of operating and adapting.

Curiosity encourages executives to ask questions to better understand how new knowledge affects their organisation, customers, and people. It's a critical component of effective leadership. Leaders must avoid becoming overly enamored with a particular plan or strategy, as the pace of change in today's environment is only increasing. Resilient leaders will be prepared with Plan B (and C). In times of transition, leaders shouldn't feel compelled to go it alone; instead, they should enlist the help of mentors, friends, coaches, trusted peers, professional colleagues, family members, and others. When you understand your own reactions to change and can better manage your emotions and reactions, your ability to adapt improves. Reframe dangerous situations as chances to learn and develop. You may use this when you're presented with change, but you can also practice this by embracing new experiences on a regular basis. Resiliency takes time to develop, but by taking action, leaders may become more flexible and effective, which will benefit themselves, their teams, and their businesses.

"Innovation separates a leader from a follower." -Steve Jobs

Adversity is the fastest way to develop and open up new chances. Adversity is necessary for progress since, without it, potential cannot be realised. Learn to see each obstacle as a chance to become the best version of yourself. Have faith that you'll always discover the solutions. However, you must first look for them. You're not required to solve the problem on your own. Use the pooled intelligence of your team and coemployees to your advantage. You can ask yourself the following questions:

- How could I handle or think about this problem differently the next time?

- Who would be the ideal companion for me to discuss this with?

There is always a bigger you inside. Don't miss a chance to discover your higher self. You do not have to continue to feel anxious or trapped, in actuality. You can always find a solution if you have a growth mentality.

Businesses are facilitated by changing organisational structures. Resilient organisations aren't scared to embrace possibilities that aren't directly related to their core business. Resilient IT executives strive to include flexibility in their business structures. Consistency, scalability, and resiliency are provided by platform teams. High-performing companies organise themselves around the work that needs to be done, relying on partner ecosystems to unbundle work while simultaneously driving innovation. At the onset of the pandemic, a customised business goods organisation saw a new potential in the marketplace to make masks and collaborated with partners to swiftly offer what would become one of the most popular products.

Changing people's positions and, occasionally, their professional identities is a common part of leading them through transformation. If you're switching from a traditional waterfall model to an agile methodology, for example, your project managers and business analysts will need to learn new skills, modify how they work, and become scrum masters and product owners, respectively. Work with your human resources employees to map out skills and reorganise if needed. An internal knowledge audit will also help you uncover knowledge gaps in this situation. A competent business leader understands the business instinctively and has extensive knowledge of customers, the industry, and competitors. Use this knowledge to create new product offers and process modifications. Make sure you're not missing anything by conducting studies and evaluating your options. Do your study and review your metrics—employees engagement, percentage of revenue change, customer happiness score, and so on—to make sure you're not missing anything. Always remember to include positive consumer input in each "change exercise."

These resilient leaders are able to function effectively, adapt rapidly, invent new methods of working, and alter their businesses in a seamless manner. Because they are so absorbed in their difficulties, leaders frequently become trapped. "Zooming out," or moving from "the dance floor to the balcony," as Ron Heifetz, Marty Linksy, and Alexander Grashow describe it in The Practice of Adaptive Leadership, gives you a broader perspective and a systemic view of the issues, and can reveal unexamined assumptions that would otherwise go undetected. Interdependencies and wider patterns become visible from this "balcony" or elevated vantage point, possibly revealing unanticipated difficulties and new solutions. This more comprehensive viewpoint allows for better resiliency and, when necessary, path adjustment. By making this dance floor-balcony change a regular practice, you may increase your capacity to perceive the larger picture and grow as a leader.

Organisations must produce leaders who can adjust themselves and their organisations to deal with challenges now. Development of resilient leadership a new leadership development framework is required. One that can be given at scale and creates resilient leaders at all levels, sooner in their careers and in the flow of their work. The new model stresses learning in the context of the organisation's business conditions, processes, and objectives, as well as quick implementation of what has been learned.

Implementing resilient leadership poses a number of challenges. Even while resilient leadership is a valuable theory, putting it into practice may be difficult. There are two key hurdles that a leader must overcome while attempting to adopt this framework: One of the most significant challenges for an resilient leader is the human instinct to resist change.

Authority figures have an impact on people. If you don't model the act of naming sensitive topics as the authority, it's doubtful that anybody else would. Your job is to keep them safe and encourage them to speak up. When they say anything that makes you uncomfortable, be interested and encourage them to elaborate on their notions. People feel a sense of shared responsibility for the overall organisation when: people offer to provide resources to help others; rewards are based at least partially on the overall organisation's performance; new ideas and insights are shared across boundaries; and people take the time to understand what others are doing in other areas of the organisation. Some authority figures value independence because it provides them with a sense of importance. The resilient leader's task is to become expendable by continually delegating work to others. Resilient leadership fosters a culture of leadership across the organisation.

Resilient leaders have strong personalities and adhere to a system of ethics and beliefs. Resilient leaders are good at generating trust, which is necessary for implementing successful solutions to adaptive difficulties. They hold themselves to the same standards that they hold others to, resulting in a culture of openness and respect. So far, you've looked at what resilient leadership is, why it's essential, and some of the concepts that underpin it. Let's take a look at a few talents that an resilient leader must possess.

- Leadership that can adapt who accept that uncertainty is an unavoidable aspect of change and are content not to have all of the answers all of the time.
- They emphasise experimenting and learning as a means of arriving at the best possible answers to a challenge.
- They are emotionally aware and do not allow personal sentiments to come in the way of making good judgments for the organisation.
- They place a high value on relationships and devote time to establishing trust and hearing diverse points of view that differ from their own.
- They recognise that change takes time and might be unpleasant.
- They are patient and persistent till they achieve their goals.
- They foster a feeling of shared purpose and values among employees so that they may make independent, self-directed decisions that are in line with the organisation's aims and strategy.

The resilient leadership philosophy emphasizes overcoming obstacles in order to achieve organisational success. This entails assisting stakeholders in navigating new and complex circumstances that arise as a result of improvement activities. When tackling any situational problem linked with a change attempt, leaders who try to take an resilient approach should consider the following characteristics, as I explained in this book on resilient leadership.

- The desired speed of change will not be achieved by the organic evolution of the tech stack. Adaptive businesses make use of technology platforms and ecosystem partners to boost their capacity to offer customer value at scale by using thin customisation layers. Platforms help innovation chains expedite the adoption of new technologies and capabilities. A major insurance organisation developed many basic technology platforms, reducing time-to-market by 21% and increasing efficiency by 19%.
- Organisations cannot afford to wait for trends to emerge before acting. Resilient businesses use data to foresee and respond to growing client demands and expectations. Resilient businesses strive to build virtuous cycles in which they can use consumer and partner information to continuously give value and spot emerging requirements. A prominent industrial manufacturing business has embedded digital capabilities into its products to increase performance, do predictive maintenance, and establish a stronger relationship and greater value for its customers.
- To allow change, you must be able to persuade others to say *"yes"* to your demands. You may reduce opposition by presenting your request as a solution that supports the stakeholders‘ vision. Being a controversial person whose requests don't regard their stakeholders is a rapid road to failure and alienation. The aim is to pique people's interest in talking about your request so you may express your ideas. If your stakeholders, on the other hand, appear indifferent, leave it alone until the dialogue and the right opportunity arise again.
- Execute each duty according to the roles, duties, and instructions you've been given until you've earned the

right to speak for others. As you earn the ability to advocate on your own behalf, be sure your actions are always in line with the purpose, vision, and objectives of those who are empowering you. Being intrapreneurial is a great way to start a business. The capacity to deliver quick, succinct, and insightful ideas to stakeholders is critical for a powerful leader's day-to-day. The manner in which you participate also influences the future possibilities for you to be welcomed. Nonetheless, your capacity to express and convince people in your business with authority is critical to your success.

- Although competent leaders are more comfortable making partial judgements and discovering gray areas within doctrine in order to achieve their goals in the near term, they nevertheless rely on chain of command direction for all of their decisions. Resilient leaders, on the other hand, are similar to intrapreneurs in that they see operational possibilities and create visions to profit from them.
- To respond to opportunities and disruptions, cross-functional teams must adjust all organisational systems, including incentives and recognition, talent management, and learning and development. Begin with your own personal knowledge and abilities. When you've found resilient leaders, search for leadership, technology, and management knowledge from outside sources to continue expanding your adaptive leadership schema. To help you scale, create a leadership team with a single leadership system attitude. Integrate organisational leadership competence and capacity into leaders' daily work flows. Integrate critical thinking, diversity, and other behavioral skills into the content and learning experience.

- A diverse attitude adaptive leadership is based on a diversity-welcoming worldview. This is not the narrow concept of diversity that frequently leads to tokenism, whether perceived or real. Real diversity tests established ways of thinking and working, and it pervades various aspects of a organisation, including three main areas: To begin, promoting the advancement of diverse people entails not just recruiting and promoting individuals of other colors or genders, but also those who think differently and challenge established standards. Second, more personalised career advancement rather than a set, standard, and linear career ladder allows for more different career pathways. Third, recruiting, onboarding, learning and development, and performance management procedures should all include the delivery of intended results.

As previously said, change frequently necessitates many stakeholders letting go of what they consider valuable or familiar. Beliefs, values, actions, identities, and ideologies may all change as a result of this. Changing any of these factors might be difficult. Resilient leaders must set their egos aside and be open to letting go of their own ideas, taking responsibility for their mistakes, and delegating power and authority in order to find the greatest possible answer to the adaptive situation at hand. For leaders, overcoming these internal struggles may be a big task.

What are some examples of how resilient leaders approach to solve a problem?

Let's take a look at a few instances of organisational issues and how an resilient leader could handle the situation. You worked in a team managed by a well-respected and admired leader a few years back. Your leader was capable, ethical, and humble, and he really cared about his people. He chose to quit the organisation due to a change in his circumstances, which disappointed practically everyone on his team. He was replaced by a new boss who had been hired from outside the organisation. There was a lot of concern about the incoming leader and how this changeover would affect all of your lives. The new leader might have stepped in and acted from a position of power. He might have viewed the move as a technical issue, with all he needed to do now being to ensure that the knowledge transfer was complete and that he was prepared to handle the business's operations. However, he knew that this method would almost certainly lead to problems down the road because he required his team's buy-in to succeed. As a result, he chose an resilient approach, first accepting that the shift would be difficult for the squad and that he would be filling enormous shoes.

Developing a leadership pipeline is critical for the organisation's long-term flexibility. When self-organising, cross-functional teams become the rule rather than the exception, innovation thrives. Top innovators create a flexible organisational structure that allows employees across the organisation to align themselves with new innovation initiatives that excite them. A flexible organisation necessitates new working methods. While organisations have typically relied on gut feelings and manager discretion when making crucial employees choices, digital leaders are increasingly turning to behavioral analytics. The goal here isn't to peek over individual employees' shoulders, but rather to examine behavior patterns to see if they match the strategic aim. This kind of knowledge may lead to significant improvements in recruiting, training, incentives, and team coordination.

Early in 2021, Forrester forecasted that one fifth of the Fortune 500's tech-laggard organisations would fail to make it through the year. Those businesses that are able to take advantage of the market's dynamism will prosper in this climate. According to Forrester, companies that have a future-fit strategy are able to restructure their basic business principles to produce and deliver in this new world. According to Forrester, companies that have a future-fit strategy are better prepared to rearrange their basic business principles to generate and deliver value to fulfill consumer expectations in this new world. And the distinction is striking. According to a Forrester assessment of prominent companies, resilient companies grew roughly three times faster than the industry average. Future-ready leaders do this by employing resilient technology, making decisions based on predictive insights, and creating a flexible organisation that can react to changing market conditions.

Resilient leadership is the deliberate evolution of a leader in real time, sometimes under difficult conditions. It will motivate you to challenge—and perhaps reject—the current quo in favor of innovative approaches. It will almost certainly be necessary to change attitudes and views, as well as to combat hesitant conduct. What steps can you take to become a more resilient leader? According to the importance of emotional intelligence, the five competences of emotional intelligence are self-awareness, self-management, social awareness, empathy, and social relationship management. To succeed in positions of power, you'll need these abilities. Resilient leaders also make fair judgments, share knowledge, retain integrity, develop others, and continue to grow throughout their lives. Adaptive challenges are problems that experts are unable to solve. They necessitate in-house tests, findings, and changes. People must accept new values and attitudes, as well as absorb the change, in order to make the adaptive jump. Resilient leaders lead with empathy, learn from their mistakes, accept change, and create conditions that benefit the greatest number of people. Resilient leadership may help authority figures see the broad picture and delegate important work back to individuals and teams during times of crisis.

Many changes entail adaptation issues that require people to develop new skills. In corporate and community transformation attempts, this is frequently disregarded. People must adapt to address challenges in order for the shift to be effective. Adapt or change is required of both leaders and individuals. Individuals must develop their own capacity to solve issues and capitalize on opportunities. Many of your greater societal crises, such as climate change, do not have a technology solution to transition from individual to systemic challenges. You need people to modify what they do until there is a technological answer, and you need to address the bigger adaptive issues involved in making these adjustments, which include, among other things, value systems and identity. Leaders must mobilise their followers to modify existing habits and build new ones.

It's easy to simplify difficult problems to make them appear less intimidating. Breaking down a difficulty into its constituent parts, for example, might make you feel more in control of the situation, but it can also restrict your perspective and mask important interdependencies, giving you a false feeling of security. Drawing comparisons from previous issues might be valuable, but it can also lead to you overlooking the particular details of the current challenge. Leaders must learn to combine their drive for action with a disciplined approach to comprehending both the fundamental problem and their own biases, rather than succumbing to the need for speedy solutions.

Resilient leaders know how to invent alternate uses of things to promote their vision, just as core and effective leaders know how to identify what should and shouldn't work. Core leadership, I feel, equals book smarts, successful leadership equals street smarts, and resilient leadership means inventiveness. To put it another way, core leaders are recognised for their competency, successful leaders for their expertise, and resilient leaders for their visions with flexible paths. The greater the level of uncertainty, the more untrainable leadership development is infused.

Resilient leadership promotes creativity, progress, and positive reactions to change. Learn about the characteristics of resilient leadership and how to use it in difficult situations. environments that are difficult to work in. You have recently been chosen to lead a organisation that has had a slew of issues in the past. The business is in financial trouble, but the environment is also an issue. Employees have little faith in the organisation's leadership. There is a lot of tension in the corporate world between different groups, including politics, gender, ethnicity, and other concerns. You are both delighted and anxious.

How can you possibly be the leader in such a difficult situation?

Many organisation problems are presented in terms of income, but the fact is that many business problems stem from unsolved difficulties in a difficult work environment. This might indicate a problem with polarisation in politics or prejudice. It might also refer to situations where different groups believe in conflicting visions for the organisation or when there is a lot of distrust and unhappiness. Let's look at resilient leadership and tactics for execution in a demanding environment to help you think about how to manage your team. Furthermore, the system's viewpoint instils accountability since employees recognise that their actions have consequences.

Resilient or adaptive leadership is critical when unexpected occurrences disrupt work or cause an urgent problem that demands the leader's attention. According to a descriptive study on management activities and decision-making, most managers spend a significant amount of time dealing with difficulties and disturbances that potentially disrupt work. A crisis is an uncommon and urgent situation with potentially significant consequences, such as serious accidents, explosions, natural catastrophes, equipment malfunctions, product flaws, supply shortages, health problems, employee strikes, sabotage, or a terrorist attack.

After a time of rapid adaptation, businesses throughout the world are considering what the new world may look like in the next few years. Both very probable trends (such as increased working from home and more e-commerce) and other high-impact trends whose future growth is considerably more unpredictable will change the world of tomorrow. Grouping these tendencies into two dimensions is a useful way to think about them: trends in economic structural and policy transformations, typified by nations and major corporations seeking to mitigate global interdependency concerns. trends in residents' long-term behavioral adjustments as consumers and employees, deriving from their early experiences of social isolation and lockdown.

As you face the expanding demands of their positions, the leaders you deal with frequently describe feeling trapped, ill-equipped, or overwhelmed. It's understandable to feel this way when our world's complexity exceeds our "complexity of thought," as Robert Kegan and Lisa Lahey describe in their book Immunity to Change. To put it another way, since the mid-1950s, computing capacity has expanded more than a trillion-fold, while our brains have remained constant. Leaders must first learn to lead themselves in order to effectively lead others in more complicated situations. Despite the fact that each leader has their own set of circumstances, we've identified six tactics that can help you grow, adapt, and overcome more complicated issues.

Leaders that are skilled in the dispositional characteristics of resiliency inspire others in the organisation or team to embrace change.

As a method of acknowledging that change has occurred and new group dynamics will emerge, they encourage contributions from others, honestly congratulate others for their innovative ideas, and make formal introductions of individuals who are new to the organisation or team. Personality-related resiliency also entails staying highly engaged during times of change – not "checking out"emotionally or physically, remaining enthusiastic and energetic, consistently and usefully contributing to new strategy brainstorming, and successfully integrating into a new team or working across new organisational boundaries. Effective leaders, on the other hand, enable the transition process to take place rather than rejecting emotions and negative reactions or being tough and rushing through change. Denial; resistance; investigation, questioning, and reaction; and, finally, commitment are common stages in change reactions. People can gain more resiliency in the face of change through this technique.

It's fine for managers to express their opposition to change—in fact, it's preferred—because suppressed emotions will ultimately arise and must be addressed. Resistance to change is natural, yet the emotional element of adaptation requires recognition and knowledge of change. When you admit your reluctance to a change, others in the organisation can help you cope with it. At the same time, it's critical to keep emotions in check, retain a sense of balance, and stay on track. The emotional component of adaptation is addressing the feelings of others. Managers should encourage employees to communicate their sentiments about a change, whether they are favorable or negative, and should not be critical of such communication. One approach to achieving this is to schedule a weekly organisational or group meeting and allow everyone to express their ideas and feelings regarding the change that is taking place and the impact it is having.

Although the necessity for leaders to be resilient is well recognised, little is known about what adaptation actually entails. If the capacity to lead and manage change is the key differentiator in today's increasingly fast-paced corporate environment, CEOs who can adapt to change rather than merely cope with it will consistently achieve exceptional results. Metathesiophobia, that's the tongue-twisting term for the dread of change, which most people will acknowledge having experienced if they're honest with themselves. Even when the change is minimal and the individual desires it, it can be unpleasant and disturbing—and hence terrifying. Fear is often accompanied by stress and resistance. Fearing and rejecting change, as well as refusing to venture into the unknown, may be fatal to leaders, their followers, and their organisations. The only thing that stays the same in today's corporate climate is change, and change is more unpredictable and complex than ever before.

Leaders frequently state that they favor transparency. What they truly mean is that they want to know what their teams are up to all of the time. Leaders who are honest about their own work—sharing information about what they're working on, bigger corporate goals, and the priorities that should direct their teams' work—are required for adaptive leadership. Of course, teams must be capable in order to be effective in solving their own problems. Employees benefit from both formal and embedded learning opportunities, such as work shadowing and job rotation, provided by great adaptive leaders. Resilient leaders don't wait for a slowdown to grow their people—they know those are rare—instead, they use busy moments to stretch and challenge team members to contribute in new ways and through new responsibilities that stretch and challenge them.

Learning is impossible without some risk and failure. While conventional leaders may seek for green lights on the dashboard progress report, resilient leaders encourage individuals to be open about where they've pushed themselves and where they may be struggling—the truth. Customers must be involved in the process for adaptive work approaches to be successful. Great adaptive leaders make it easier for customers to participate. Consumers' expectations are defined, opportunities and workplaces where customers may be present are provided, and customers are given the time they require.

Working on one project at a time, for example, is an important aspect of resiliency. Leaders must sometimes push back on the business to ensure that adaptive teams are not overburdened and can thrive by prioritising projects and outcomes. Performance is measured by adaptive leaders. Measurement, monitoring, and management are all intertwined. Great adaptive leaders encourage teams to measure their own results in addition to tracking their own measures. They track factors like meeting time, number of projects, customer happiness, team trust, and more, in addition to velocity, the gold standard of adaptive measurement. They know how the team is doing so they can provide feedback, eliminate roadblocks, and create possibilities for growth.

Feedback is an important aspect of adaptive development. Great resilient leaders provide feedback while also empowering their teams to provide and accept input. They assist the team in maintaining contact with the organisation in order to obtain critical feedback from internal customers and the organisation as a whole. Resilient leaders serve as mentors and coaches for the teams they manage. Because resiliency is a new method of working in most organisations, outstanding adaptive leaders must educate the rest of the organisation on work procedures, eliminate barriers, and establish team boundaries. Working as a team, for example, is an important aspect of adaptive.

For teams, resilient leadership necessitates new levels of empowerment, enablement, and development. Adaptive teams are learning new work practices at the same time as executives who are ensuring success in the new adaptive environment. You will not last long if you are unable to adapt to change. This is becoming increasingly critical as the pace of change accelerates. To allow faster and better resiliency to change, a leader must comprehend not only the people around them, but also themselves.

- What exactly is the resiliency problem?
- What stands in the way of resiliency?
- How can quick resiliency be made possible?

When it comes to this, look to visionary and transformational leadership for inspiration. Leaders who put in time during a disruption achieve cost-effective results with long-term benefits. Resilient leaders put their followers first. Resilient leaders inspire their employees to recognise change and respond to it with easy solutions. They assist others in completing *"the work"* required to overcome the obstacles. Great leaders build strong, dependable, and flexible teams by utilising this adaptive talent.

Leadership is a skill that can be learned and used to solve a variety of problems in the world. It's not the same as being in a position of power. Because it conflates leadership with authority and positional power, the area of leadership—how it is regarded and perceived—is frequently complex. You know this because you grumble about those in positions of power failing to lead. Leadership may be practiced by anybody, with or without authority. The civil rights movement is a fantastic example of strong leaders who had a huge influence while having little institutional power.

Hence, If you adopt the usual route to tackling this problem, you may explore the following options:

- Perhaps you should provide extra bonuses and advantages to your staff.
- Perhaps you should give them a significant raise above their existing pay.
- Perhaps your managers need to work on improving his or her management abilities and motivating employees.

This, however, is not how resilient leadership approaches a situation like this. The HR department elected to go deeper into the source of the problem, involving the entire senior management team in the investigation to see whether monetary rewards and other incentives were the true cause or whether something else was at play. The new manager proceeded to solicit new ideas from the staff on a regular basis. His team quickly came to trust and admire him for pushing intra-team collaboration to new levels. Over the course of his career, he effectively led the squad through ups and downs and experienced success.

Task management is a strength of resilient leaders. After examining each individual's distinctive abilities and strengths, they allocate the appropriate individuals to the proper jobs. Resilient leaders empower their teams by providing them with tools and chances to improve their professional skills. Resilient leaders are skilled at detecting nonverbal clues and interpreting their colleagues' emotions. This ability enables them to comprehend others and steer their actions accordingly. Resilient leaders strive to get the greatest results in the simplest way feasible. They have the ability to bend or violate current structural rules to achieve the desired effects.

You can learn to be both an observer and a participant at the same time, fortunately. When you're at a meeting, practice by monitoring what's going on as it happens—even if you're a part of it. Examine the interactions to observe how people's attention to one another varies, whether it's supporting, thwarting, or listening. Keep an eye out for people's body language. When you make a point, fight the urge to sit on the edge of your seat, ready to defend what you've said. After you talk, a simple method like moving your chair a few inches away from the table may give you the real and metaphorical space you need to become an observer.

Leaders encourage others to reconsider their own priorities and examine any inconsistencies in their value system. Contradictions are usually resolved by placing them out of sight. When people in positions of leadership ask difficult questions and point out inconsistencies, they get neutralised. Effective leaders recognise and expect losses in the course of their work. Many individuals with strong ideas and moral convictions have a tendency to discount others who disagree with them rather than see the good in the opposing system. Effective leaders must be able to talk compassionately about the losses that individuals, organisations, and communities will suffer, as well as recognise the nobility in opposing systems.

Resilient leadership promotes creativity, progress, and positive reactions to change. Rajib has recently been chosen to lead a hospitality firm that has had a slew of issues in the past. The business is in financial trouble, but the environment is also an issue. Employees have little faith in the company's leadership. There is a lot of tension in the corporate world between different groups, including politics, gender, ethnicity, and other concerns. Rajib is both delighted and anxious. How can he possibly be the leader in such a difficult situation? Many organisational problems are presented in terms of income, but the fact is that many business problems stem from unsolved difficulties in a difficult work environment. This might indicate a problem with polarisation in politics or prejudice.

It might also refer to situations where different groups believe in conflicting visions for the organisation or when there is a lot of distrust and unhappiness. Let's look at adaptable leadership and tactics for execution in a demanding environment to help Rajib think about how to manage his team. Rajib has recently joined an organisation that has been struggling in a constantly changing sector. Disruptors have transformed the way people travel, and it's having an impact on the company's bottom line. Rajib wishes to make a change in the organisation so they can respond rapidly to customer needs and industry changes. Resilient leadership is one technique to do this. This entails building an atmosphere in which all workers are empowered to make decisions and respond to issues both inside and outside the firm via innovation and continual development.

Resilient leaders are emotionally aware, which means they're aware of how they're feeling and why; and self-reflective, which means they're prepared to examine their own reasons. They are committed to self-improvement, which means they are always looking for ways to improve their job. These factors are important, but adaptable leaders are also able to let go of control and give their people more liberty. What about Rajib, though? There are so many issues in his company that he fears he will have to clamp down and be a stronger leader. He is concerned that granting employees authority would exacerbate the company's squabbling and divisions. Resilient leadership is most commonly used in businesses with a positive climate, but it may also be used in adverse situations. In fact, resilient leadership may be utilised to transform a toxic workplace into a healthier one.

Rajib is all in if resilient leadership can turn the firm around while simultaneously improving the company's social culture. But how is she going to accomplish it? Rajib has a number of options for implementing resilient leadership in her difficult job. The following are some of them:

- Rajib must figure out exactly what he needs to do. This entails recognising the industry's external difficulties that are harming the bottom line. However, it also entails recognising the internal issues affecting the company's culture. Perhaps his staff are insecure about their employment. Some of the tensions might be alleviated by adding job stability. Perhaps there isn't a clear protocol in place at the firm for reporting prejudice.
- Rajib must identify and address any obstacles to his achievement. A resilient leader may terminate a failing initiative before it has a chance to prosper. This may not sit well with certain team members, resulting in a schism among the organisation's members. Discord is an impediment to successful transformation.

You have an excellent knowledge of your feelings and the feelings of people around you if you have high

Emotional Intelligence. You can respond to your team in a fair, calm, and compassionate manner if you have acquired emotional intelligence. Of course, there are many aspects to emotional intelligence, and being sympathetic, searching for emotional reactions, respecting people's feelings, and adjusting your actions to their feelings can bring you a long way in this area.

There are benefits and drawbacks to resilient leadership, just as there are to other leadership techniques. Change is unavoidable. A resilient leader isn't surprised by change. Instead, this leader has put in place procedures and tactics to deal with problems as they emerge. When a resilient leader is present, at least one backup plan is always easily available. As the world reopens, more of their hand sanitising systems are likely to be acquired. The tale of ChargedUp exemplifies resilient leadership at its finest. Things were not going to be the same for the squad, so they swiftly adapted to their new surroundings. For the resilient leader, rules serve as a guideline rather than a strict manner of doing things. This leader is intent on attaining the best possible result in the most efficient manner possible. It may even become clear that the present regulations aren't working for the company and need to be changed. Every resilient leader should have the following characteristics: the capacity to relate organizational change to the core values, abilities, and dreams of the stakeholders engaged.

The key to creating resilient leadership is to cultivate a development attitude. Your capacity to react nimbly to difficulties is what we call resilience. Change is necessary for adaptability, and constructive change promotes progress.

CHAPTER TWO

The Impact Of Resilient Leadership On People In Turbulent Times

"Before you are a leader, success is all about growing yourself. When you become a leader, success is all about growing others." —Jack Welch

Resilience is what separates successful people from failed ones. While failed individuals persistently dwell on their failures and are reluctant to explore and experiment more, successful people know how to recover from difficulties, disappointments, and failures. In the midst of the layoff upheaval in contrast to other leaders, resilient leaders cause things to fall into place. They don't put the blame on the situation. Instead, they accept accountability and make an attempt to shape events and results. They don't dwell on their previous transgressions. Instead, they look for solutions to their problems. They are not issues; they are part of the answers. Any Tom, Dick, or Harry may become a hero, star, or leader when things are going well. When the going gets tough, thougher get going, it calls for strong leaders who can face the difficulties and adjustments head-on. When the ship is sailing through the storm to reach the beach safely, the true leaders emerge. Resilient leaders with the courage and vision to face the issue are needed in difficult times. The genuine stars, heroes, and leaders emerge during storms. For some leaders who have a lot of potential, problems might be blessings in disguise.

What exactly is leadership resilience?

Resilience is still a crucial quality of effective leaders, whether or not there is a pandemic. Resilience is the human ability and process of adapting in the face of difficulty, trauma, and disruptive events, according to the American Psychological Association (APA) it is the capacity to "bounce back" after setbacks, to put it simply. These traits are displayed in the workplace by resilient leaders who are able to operate under extreme stress, embrace challenging changes, and put forward creative and flexible solutions. These leaders can also overcome significant obstacles without resorting to destructive actions or hurting other people. This comprehensive approach enables them to work closely with their values and with a feeling of empathy, another essential component of leadership. It is this true and enduring sort of leadership that brings value to workplaces and to the lives of employees.

Leadership becomes more difficult when competing values exist.

Leaders who are resilient display a positive outlook and have the foresight to handle both the expected and unexpected, frequently working with newly reduced budgets. Leaders must be able to quickly change priorities without losing sight of the broader picture, since pressure is something that comes with the territory. They must also comprehend that sometimes the finest leadership tactic is to confess that you don't have all the answers. They must also know when to consult specialists to ensure that all business choices are supported by fact rather than by cognitive leadership bias.

Resilient leaders recognise and embrace adversity.

Not all businesses suffered during the epidemic; in fact, some businesses were fortunate enough to be in the right place at the right time. For example, "work from home" businesses and e-commerce giants had managed to stay afloat thanks to a strong emphasis on resilience, financial stability, and contingency preparation. There were, however, some that had strategically leveraged the crisis to develop their organisation's strategies for growth. In every case, these businesses had proven an exceptional capacity to adapt.

- Accepting failure is the first step in becoming more resilient. Accepting failure is not the same as giving up or quitting.
- Organisations must accept new ideas and make adjustments as a result. It is best to engage new minds and take advantage of their recent learning to ensure an influx of ideas. Employees must also be taught how to think and act strategically.
- Accepting setbacks as a temporary situation is to invite failure. A stepping stone to knowledge It's all about seizing opportunities to advance.

- Accepting different ideas from various people in business is one way to build a culture that is receptive to failure.
- Keeping an eye on weather change energises consumers and provides incentives to try new products or services.
- When we stumble or make a mistake, there is always a lesson to be learned. As it is said, "What doesn't kill us makes us stronger."
- Be upbeat about the lesson and understand that what matters is that we can fill the glass, not whether it is half full or half empty. It's excellent that mistakes, blunders, and losses occur. What did it teach you? The plan is to stand up and continue moving. There is always another route.
- Encourage innovation by researching new ideas ahead of time and supporting innovative corporate cultures.
- Develop a solid digital transformation plan to keep up with technological improvements and to stay ahead of any possible disruption.
- Instilling learning is another technique to make an organisation more resilient. The rapidity of change, as well as the influence of fast globalisation, is a problem for resilient organisations.
- Resilient organisation to stay one step ahead of their industry's competitors. It is critical to behave effectively and efficiently in addition to working quickly and harder.
- It is critical to promote responsibility in order to achieve adaptation. It's always simpler to blame success on hard work and blame failure on bad luck, but resilient businesses prioritise cultivating and developing a culture of self-accountability.

- The sense of responsibility guarantees that each member completes their obligations with dedication. It fosters a culture of trust and assists the organisation in avoiding "cya" techniques and blame games.
- This gives front-line staff the perspective of top executives, which can help them make rapid judgments when they're needed the most.
- Adapting to change is what makes us useful, relevant, and on the cutting edge of innovation. Failure, learning, accountability, and change are all things that an resilient organisation embraces.
- Resilient organisations strive to provide proactive innovation, satisfy consumers and other stakeholders, and lead with appreciation and wisdom in the corporate environment.

Any resilient and future-ready organisation will have these characteristics. This will allow organisations to respond more swiftly to changes in client needs, technological developments, and disturbing competition than organisations that rely solely on size and efficiency. Many other internal and external factors may limit an organisation's capacity to adapt, but greater planning and transformation may serve as a roadmap for executives wishing to avoid the same blunders that have brought other businesses to their knees. The majority of leaders I've encountered might become more resilient if they gave themselves a bit more leeway. To put it another way, how can you mentor, care for, and create space for people on your team if you aren't caring for yourself? I advise scheduling a 30-minute self-care exercise for the leader once a week.

Be sure not to fight the thought or sensation; instead, confront it head-on. It vanishes as soon as you accept it and welcome it.

The first method breathing exercises is excellent for removing undesirable ideas and emotions at the time they arise. However, the next method will help you if you wish to gradually diminish them. Choose a quiet spot to relax where you won't be disturbed for five minutes. Set the timer on your smartwatch or phone for five minutes. Put your eyes closed and concentrate solely on your breathing as you inhale and exhale softly.

Utilise the "five-ten-five" breathing technique, in which you inhale to the count of five, hold for ten counts, and then exhale to the five-count. Ensure that you are breathing from the diaphragm as well. When your stomach pushes out on the inhale and moves in on the exhale, you know you are doing this. This method offers two advantages. You are first teaching your mind to quit talking nonstop. Second, it will effectively lower your heart rate and increase the amount of oxygen in your blood, which may have sedative-like effects. Your heart, mind, and whole central nervous system will quickly become calm.

This method of breathing aids in controlling the area of your brain in charge of the fight, flight, and freeze reactions. You are less likely to encounter these moods when under stress if you perform this exercise frequently. Do this exercise twice a day, first in the morning and then at night. If you pick the same time every day, such as just when you get up and right before bed, it will be simpler to develop this habit. Additionally, use it to regain control if you notice things slipping during the day.

"You are not constrained by limiting ideas and failures from the past, being in the present is empowering."

Being in the now is effective because you are not constrained by limiting beliefs, burdened by mistakes in the past, or concerned about the future. Instead, when you are in the present moment, you have complete access to the power of your mind. To illustrate the importance of being in the moment, think about professional athletes. Why are they able to perform well one day and poorly the next? Did their abilities mysteriously vanish? Consider a tennis player who is preparing to serve the ball. They notice that it is break time when they glance up. Their attention shifts abruptly to the future and what may occur if they miss the point. That implies using less effort and concentration to hit the ball. But what if they stopped thinking about the scoreboard and started living in the present? They accomplish this by concentrating solely on serving the ball. They are so concentrated that they could even be made aware of an opponent's minor movement in a certain direction by their thinking. They may now alter their serve and win the point with ease thanks to this.

In this manner, great players win games on a regular basis. They understand the effectiveness of keeping one's thoughts and attention in the present. Watching the scoreboard will always pull you out of the present. Gaining access to the power of the present moment is essential for leaders who want to achieve. It also signifies that you no longer require resilience. This is due to the fact that staying in the present moment naturally results in resilience.

What are some ways that you may practise being in the present?

Aim to go forward one step at a time. Just like a tennis player focuses their attention on playing one shot at a time, go from one instant to the next. Start by focusing on a simple task you carry out every day, such as speaking with a team member. This gets more intriguing the more you play with it. Because you are putting all of yourself into the work and not just a portion of it, every time you do this, you will gain more understanding and clarity. Both your conscious and creative unconscious minds are there in each and every one of you.

Technical and resilient challenges: what are they?

Technical difficulties require that one or more specialists with strong reputations are recruited to solve the issue" and that a predetermined acceptable remedy is already available. Since leaders are frequently familiar with technical issues, implementing the solutions already in their toolbox is typically all that is required to quickly resolve them.

On the other hand, resilient problems go beyond the leader's expertise and skill set, necessitating a swift analysis of the problem, the formulation of a strategy for its mitigation, the mobilisation of talent, and eventually the taking of certain risks in order to carry out the strategy. The adaptation difficulties for the majority of us might range from a significant business upheaval to a worldwide epidemic.

Leaders that make the effort to understand their team members gain a lot of insight about the skills exhibited by the team members. When an adaptation challenge approaches, this storehouse of outstanding abilities and experiences may be helpful. Knowing the talent available to them, the team's leader's job is to enable the team to use their knowledge and practical experience.

The road to empowerment is easy to follow. Be open about the difficulties with adaptation. Give employees the freedom to troubleshoot their resilient difficulties and a place to communicate about them. Get out of the way of the outstanding grassroots projects that are having an impact. This is most crucial.

What are the elements of resilient leadership required in VUCCAD business world?

The resilient leader is aware that going through change can be difficult. As a result, he or she is able to anticipate and deal with any hesitant conduct from colleagues. An awareness that major change is a slow process that necessitates tenacity and the capacity to withstand the pressure that goes along with it. Only through a shift in attitudes and policy changes will you be able to sustain change and grow. However, changing people's attitudes, opinions, and perspectives is frequently more challenging than brushing a cat's teeth. You have to be slightly unfaithful to your history.

For instance, accepting the reality that your present marketing strategies are unproductive is a prerequisite for implementing a new marketing plan. The majority of top executives are reluctant to abandon enduring practises that helped launch their businesses. The advantages that can come from using new techniques might be hampered, though, if you keep to your old habits.

I've learned from my personal leadership experience that empathy may be either natural or acquired. Many people must strive to develop it, while some are born with it. In any case, empathy is crucial when faced with adaptation problems. First and foremost, the team members need to feel that the leader is concerned about the difficulties they are going through. A brief conversation over the water cooler for 30 seconds, a fruit basket delivery, or an office message do not constitute "care." To show that they care, leaders must engage in active listening and ask the types of questions that encourage team members to be completely honest about their worries and failures in the face of resilient hurdles. It requires time and an embodied presence to actively listen.

Empowerment must, of course, become the norm before the resilient difficulty appears. Every day, a capable leader cultivates empowerment. The primary role of the leader is to provide optimism when everything else fails. Teams that are encouraged to think beyond the resilient task will always be better prepared to handle the problem's volatility. There are various practical approaches for leaders to demonstrate to their employees and themselves that they are resilient. Let's look more closely at these crucial elements for becoming a resilient leader and how to put them into practise. Every resilient leader should have specific qualities, such as:

- You must continually adapt to the times in order to become a resilient leader, and this goes for your skill set as well as your entire worldview. You may enable yourself to grow and evolve naturally by choosing to be a lifelong learner by reading, research, enrolling in professional courses or credentials, or just conversing with others.

- The capacity to connect organisational transformation to the fundamental talents, aspirations, and values of the concerned stakeholders.
- The ability to foster an environment that values diversity of opinion and uses that information to the benefit of the organisation.
- Being proactive, searching for chances, and devoting the resources required to seize them. Recognising their errors and altering or giving up on unsuccessful tactics.
- Be deliberate about taking lessons from a variety of situations, from risks and experiments to chances and accomplishments.
- By embracing learning, we may better manage losses and come out the other side stronger, smarter, and more equipped to handle whatever challenges lie ahead. Additionally, it enables us to advance with a fresh perspective and perhaps even new values learned from the experience.
- Being willing to try new things and take risks supporting and promoting employee innovation.
- This leadership style is all about trying new things, learning new things, and making plenty of changes all around your business.
- The fact that resilient leadership creates the conditions for various types of opposition raises another difficulty. This could be from customers, partners in the business, or employees members.
- Resilient leadership offers significant benefits despite requiring a lot of work. According to reliable data, organisations that are resilient see enormous advantages in both financial and operational terms. Even during times of turbulence, they can withstand storms and succeed.

- Leaders will need to know how to develop strong, cohesive teams, despite the evident difference between team members at the office and those working from home, in order to make this work effectively while preserving productivity and efficiency.

Active listening cannot be achieved through texting. Mutual trust is fostered when the leader demonstrates empathy. Consider how a team member who has consistently succeeded on the team suddenly starts making mistakes or speaking rudely to the other team members. Saying, "Raise the quality of your work or there will be repercussions," is a common leadership directive. On the other side, a compassionate approach involves the leader saying, "I realise you're hurting right now." What can I do to help you? The latter strategy fosters trust. If the leader hopes to guide their team through and past the adaptation obstacles, trust is crucial. The team does not necessarily need to share the leader's perspective on the resilient issue in order to be trusted.

Creating resilient leaders and teams probably depends most on developing trustworthy connections. Building trust through constructive connections can help you win the team's support while you're working in an environment that calls for a lot of risk-taking and change. This includes relying on and connecting with people, which isn't a sign of weakness, in addition to letting others trust you. This is primarily because it denotes self-awareness and your ability to trust yourself and others.

Establishing a daily goal to connect with at least one team member can help leaders develop trust. Even if you're depressed and anxious, talking to someone about your ideas might help you find a solution or feel better. It does imply that the team has faith that the leader has their best interests in mind, regardless of how they choose to handle the task. That is how trust is developed. In the effort to overcome adaptation barriers, empowerment works in conjunction with empathy.

It takes understanding life to be a leader since, in general, not many things will go your way. Gain the patience to comprehend other people's capacity to learn at their own rate while accepting failure as your best friend, learning to go with the flow, and never giving up on yourself. You need to be resilient to various kinds of cultures and individuals in order to be resilient. Changing one's viewpoint on issues is one tactic a leader may use to become more resilient. The game-changer, though, is not considering the issue intractable. A leader has control over how they understand situations and react to them. Making future-focused projections and decisions now can help you make wise choices and develop resilience.

Resilient leaders are aware that maintaining the vital connections they have made through trust depends on good communication. These leaders purposefully communicate with their teams to ensure that everyone knows the goals and tactics and can work well together.

Resilience requires being aware of unpleasant feelings, embracing them rather than fighting them, and being compassionate to oneself when things are tough. Asking, "What would a close friend who cares about me profoundly say to me right now?" is a useful trick to accomplish this.

In today's workplace, change is the only constant, so it requires a strong leader to take on the various issues that face their enterprises. They distinguish themselves by conveying a distinct vision and a spirit that motivates action, frequently serving as change agents themselves.

Risk-taking is a necessary component of becoming a change agent. A leader that exhibits resilience will fearlessly test out new concepts because they know that the sooner you fail and learn, the sooner you can do it correctly the next time. It's preferable to remaining motionless, being stuck in a rut, and falling behind in a dynamic environment. According to Facebook's renowned creator, Mark Zuckerberg, "the only approach that is sure to fail in a world that is changing incredibly rapidly is not taking chances." In these challenging times, leaders have a larger duty, and they need to be tough to triumph. The smartest and most resilient people are aware that investing in leadership development solutions benefits both them personally and their organisation as a whole. The next time you consider how to improve your organisation, focus on the resilient traits you can provide your employees; it just might make you both stronger and better.

Adherents of the resilient leadership method must demonstrate a few essential traits. Just few of the most crucial characteristics for resilient leaders are listed below. Leaders frequently exhibit resilience in a variety of ways in a professional setting, including:

- Resilience, is what gives people the psychological fortitude to handle stress and adversity. People's ability to draw on their mental reserves of strength in difficult situations is what keeps them from crumbling. Resilient people, according to psychologists, are better equipped to withstand hardship and recover from misfortune.
- Resilient people tackle challenges head-on rather than giving up or using unhealthy coping mechanisms to avoid them.

- Even in the face of extreme or stressful circumstances that are completely unexpected or out of the ordinary, they remain unflappable.
- By adopting a "test and learn" approach and being outspoken about doing so, leaders may increase their resilience (thus serving as role models). If we assume that most strategies are experiments, then "negative" results are less unpleasant; instead, they turn into either disproven theories or signs that the settings may be changed to conduct another experiment.
- They have a high level of tolerance for ambiguity and uncertainty and can easily adjust to these novel situations.
- They take care of their own physical and emotional health because they understand that performing at their best requires a clean bill of health.
- They always communicate in a calm and certain manner, which inspires faith in their leadership.
- They have an excellent grasp of reality because they can put mistakes or failures into perspective and because they set attainable objectives.
- Try out a few alternative strategies. One size rarely fits everyone in a dynamic setting. Instead of consistently using the same strategy, brainstorm with your team new ways to be innovative and solve challenges. It might be intimidating to take on leadership challenges, and you could be tempted to stick with a tried-and-true strategy, but the resilient approach forces you to think creatively whenever changes are feasible.
- Leaders who continue to grow and master their emotional intelligence will become more resilient. This expertise results from reflection, asking for feedback, and our dedication to improvement.

- Flexibility is a soft talent you use to solve resilient difficulties in your workplace in whatever ways appear appropriate at the time. It is one of the fundamental concepts of resilient leadership.
- The collaborative nature of resilient leadership is key. Seek out opportunities to consult your coemployees before making a decision. Even if you might believe you have the answer to an issue, working in collaboration with other stakeholders to discover a special solution can frequently result in more innovative and practical solutions than imposing a decision from the top down.
- Resilient corporate executives must always be willing to accept organisational change. This frequently entails reaching out to all team members in order to find potential answers to new problems rather than relying just on your own knowledge. A collaborative and inquisitive mindset is advantageous for the resilient leadership paradigm.
- Because resilient work necessitates a higher level of creativity, it might put more stress on employees. Make careful to offer rewards for choosing the less-traveled path as a leader. Treat the members of your team more as partners than as subordinates for the sake of organisational fairness. Show compassion and care to every person of your workforce.
- To handle technical issues in difficult circumstances, a high level of resourcefulness is required. You can lead your team in any situation by fusing your leadership abilities with a wealth of problem-solving expertise.
- What isn't working, let rid of. The resilient leadership paradigm emphasises attempting new ideas as well as letting go of the past.

- Divide tasks and simplify processes to increase efficiency. Establish healthy routines both at work and outside of it.
- You can also use your support system as a sounding board for new ideas and get insightful advice from a variety of different perspectives.
- Optimism is a key component of leadership, and resilient leaders frequently exude confidence and optimism in all they do.
- Examine any procedures that you believe aren't helping your business in a proactive manner. A self-correction will unavoidably happen if you regularly review your organisation's methods in the interest of optimization. Better solutions will eventually take the place of less suitable ones.
- Putting some distance between yourself and the problem you are facing will help you see the bigger picture and consider different solutions.
- Before acting, take a moment to clear your thoughts, stop yourself from reacting without thinking, and give yourself time to consider your options. Once your mind is clear and your course of action is known, take action.

Waiting on external drives to "motivate you" will never outlast intrinsic motivation. You'll become more resilient if you have internal motivation and a driving force. You will just "go for it!" without giving it a second thought. Instead of debating whether you should or shouldn't do something, use your energy to carry it through.

Fortunately, resilience is a talent that can be learned and is not inherent (something you either have or don't). The purpose of the next part is to assist present and aspiring leaders in creating a strategy for their professional growth that will enable them to become more resilient in today's chaotic and demanding environment.

Robert Noyce, a co-founder of Intel, reportedly remarked that optimism is "a crucial component of invention." How else could the person choose adventure over safety, change over staying in secure places? Resilient CEOs have the ability to see past the macroeconomic climate when things are not looking good and look for possibilities to succeed. These leaders typically have the capacity to motivate people around them to share their vision for the future because they have a larger perspective, are long-term thinkers, and play the long game.

But in order to become a resilient leader, this optimism must be supported with realism. Objectives should be S.M.A.R.T., according to the employment platform. Indeed, since they "guarantee that both leaders and teams flourish by accomplishing their goals and experiencing a sense of success" (specific, measurable, achievable, relevant, time-based).

You may conserve a lot of energy and maintain your resilience by increasing your emotional intelligence and becoming aware of how you respond to stimuli. Remind yourself that you always have the choice whether to respond to anything or not and that everything is neutral unless you give it significance. Practice awareness to distance yourself from the feeling, and balance your job with outside activities and exercise.

Micromanagement, or the belief that you must perform every duty personally, is not a quality of resilient leadership. Many managers are reluctant to delegate because they worry about losing control of crucial activities, missing vital deadlines, or witnessing a drop in quality. On the other hand, assisting team members in reaching their full potential on their own is essential for you to succeed as a manager.

One of the most crucial abilities any leader can have is the ability to delegate. However, not every activity can be assigned, so it requires practise to become proficient at recognising which duties to delegate, when, and to whom. Successful delegation frees leaders from time-consuming and/or repetitive operational activities so they can devote that time to strategic planning and other non-delegatable responsibilities.

An open mind and a can-do attitude are necessary to develop into an resilient leader. As you work to use resilient leadership techniques in your working life, keep the following in mind: Recognise that change is coming. Throughout your work, you'll unavoidably run against a lot of resilient obstacles; be ready for them in advance. When the need comes, a corporate environment that is prepared for change can rapidly and successfully adopt solutions.

Delegating is different from merely assigning someone else your menial responsibilities. You may still have some control by giving your outsourced jobs the following structure:

- Talk about deadlines and schedules.
- Decide on a timetable for checkpoints where you will assess the project's progress.
- Make any required changes.
- Examine all of the work that has been submitted.
- Give the proper individual credit so that their hard work gets recognised.
- Create healthy habits.

Since the beginning of the global health crisis, which brought to light how hybrid working may help individuals construct a healthy lifestyle around their work, the concerns of work-life balance have become more and more important. A regular physical fitness programme prepares leaders for the cerebral and intellectual obstacles they encounter, according to this Forbes article on the daily rituals of outstanding leaders.

Resilient leaders understand they must maintain their body and mind in top shape to perform at their best in business, whether that means accepting business calls while out for a brisk morning walk or preparing for a marathon.

The best resilience technique I've ever used is to first establish your North Star (also known as your life's mission and purpose—your overarching objectives). Reverse-engineer the steps that will get you to these overarching objectives, and frame challenges as "stepping stones" that will help you get there. Finally, thank God every day for every stepping stone you've discovered.

When our bodies are balanced, it is much simpler to feel robust. Make sure to get enough sleep, eat a healthy diet, and exercise so that your body and mind can face problems with composure and clarity. We are more resilient when we are healthy and well-rested.

Remember that everything in business is simply a game. Similar to the games we dreamed up as children on the playground, it is a sophisticated social game. There are "good men" and "bad guys" who do business using currencies that are just as arbitrary as marbles or Pogs in terms of their value. Everyone wants to improve their position, and most people are aware that following the rules is the best way to do so. Play the game, then.

The resilient leadership strategy emphasises both taking calculated risks and doing so. Try new things, but keep it in check by determining which problem-solving techniques are currently working as well as they can. A win-win situation is achieved by balancing risks with knowledge.

There is an almost infinite variety of ways that various leaders have used, as you can see when you look at instances of resilient leadership theory in action. This is so because the whole strategy is based on opposing the status quo and conventional limitations. Recognise the significance of conventions and time-honored procedures, but keep in mind that you may always veer off the path if a better option emerges.

"No one is an island, according to the saying, and the greatest leaders are aware that they cannot accomplish greatness on their own."

Working in a team and an organisation is undoubtedly a necessary ability at every level of a organisation, but this specifically refers to a network of people you trust to be your support network. Developing into a resilient leader merely entails greater problem-solving skills. It does not mean that difficulties magically disappear. Therefore, talking about your issues with coemployees, friends, your spouse, or a family member might make you feel better about them as well as like you have someone to talk to.

Changing your leadership paradigm to be more responsive to emerging problems is known as "Resilient Leadership." Generally speaking, resilient leadership places a strong emphasis on the readiness to experiment and try new tactics to determine what works best rather than relying on conventional techniques to address technical issues. As a result, to navigate the difficulties your organisation may encounter, this leadership style calls for a willingness to take calculated risks, a constant level of curiosity, and a collaborative attitude.

Work on becoming more conscious of your thoughts and feelings every day, especially during intense periods. Take note of how your demeanour and actions change as well as how your body alters in response to various events. Recognise your triggers. The more self-aware you are, the easier it will be for you to anticipate and later manage your emotions and behaviours under trying circumstances. When worries are conquered and your self-confidence is built, personal resilience emerges. The most important traits are resiliency, emotional stability, and self-efficacy, or head, heart, and gut. The chances of someone displaying more resilience are reduced if any of these are undeveloped. These elements assist in overcoming fear and enable the leader to have a winning mentality.

Indian leaders perceive a skills shortage as their biggest danger going forward. Leaders in India are quite confident in their efforts to get ready for upcoming technological developments, but few think they are ready to face and overcome the skills shortage dilemma. Due to a dearth of crucial skills and fast technological development, Indian leaders will be put to the test during the next 12 to 18 months. According to the Global Leadership Monitor India 2022 by a global leadership advisory and executive search organisation, as many as 79% of leaders in India view the availability of talent and skills as the most urgent threat to organisational health over the next 12 to 18 months (from a list of 20 threats), while a further 58% cite technological change. And although 86% of Indian executives express high confidence in their efforts to get ready for impending technology developments, only 53% think they are ready for the prospect of a skills shortage.

24 Indian leaders were among the 1,590 CEOs that were polled by the organisation. Indian leaders are well-prepared to handle the fast technological changes they are facing, but the devil is often in the details of how change is implemented. The leadership team's capacity to engage with their leadership and develop clear succession plans is emerging as a key differentiator. On the other hand, retaining top talent, including next-gen leaders, remains problematic. A certain two-third of Next-Gen and C-suite leaders in India, according to the research, would switch employers given the proper chance. While job development was listed as the main motivation, a closer examination of this reveals more nuance: a constant search for greater responsibility as well as a need for a stronger feeling of personal connection to a sense of purpose and passion appear to drive this.

It is crucial for resilient leadership to rise to the top of the list of sought-after talents in the workplace, especially in light of unstable markets, supply chain bottlenecks, and the World Bank's prediction that global GDP would slow in 2022 from 5.5%.

Additionally, majority of leaders are open to considering taking on a new position inside their present organisation, demonstrating that the motivation is to advance and fulfil one's purpose rather than to leave. According to the report, organisations can harness the full potential of next-generation employees across longer cycles by cultivating a culture of trust and organised engagement. The following key steps to support leadership retention in order to help organisations develop teams of transformational leaders who can meet today's challenges and foresee the digital, economic, and political trends that are reshaping the global business environment:

- Early and frequent development and communication of succession plans implementing strong and motivating growth strategies for employees members at all levels.
- A quickly shifting set of goalposts that constantly gauges employee expectations.

The resilient model is built on the first principle, which is also known as climbing on the balcony. This concept calls for leaders to step back and evaluate their situation, using the metaphor of being on a balcony and viewing the larger picture. Leaders may analyse the situation, see how various people and groups are responding to difficulties, and develop deliberate methods to deal with problems by climbing onto the balcony. A typical mistake is to recognise progress in one area while ignoring problems in another. This may be avoided by taking the full picture into account.

The capacity to recognise resilient difficulties is the second resilient leadership tenet. This requires recognising problems, assessing circumstances, comprehending the sources of resistance, and overcoming obstacles to goal achievement. The capacity to swiftly distinguish between technical issues and the less evident but frequently more complicated resilient challenges is a crucial component of this notion. Technical issues, as their name suggests, are simpler to resolve and have established fixes. This can include evidence-based therapies with well-known patient outcomes for practitioners. Resilient problems are far more complicated and frequently take both individual and group views, beliefs, and values into account. This is comparable to the idea of patient-centered care, which plans a course of treatment by taking into consideration each patient's values and viewpoints.

People's focus can easily alter after significant shifts. This is especially true when adjusting to change necessitates adopting a new style of thinking and confronting core values or beliefs. Resilient leaders are focused and courageous enough to broach delicate subjects in order to meet changing circumstances and change cultures.

This theory takes into account the fact that most individuals react more positively when they can influence decisions and the way their job is done. Resilient leaders are aware of when to become involved and give guidance, as well as when to take a backseat and let others doing the actual job consider problems and put them into practice. This is particularly true in the healthcare industry, where there are many highly skilled experts who are used to exercising critical judgement and making quick decisions.

All employees need to be resilient, but they shouldn't be allowed to face challenges alone. Instead, organisations must foster a culture of shared accountability for resilience. First and foremost, leaders need to recognise when their thinking slips into two pitfalls: believing that resilience is a personality feature that some employees possess and others do not, and stigmatising the genuine feelings that employees experience when faced with difficulties. The next three questions that executives should ask themselves are:

- Can the hardship that employees are going through be lessened or eliminated?
- Are all employees dealing with this difficulty in the same way?
- What role can I play in fostering employee resilience, furthermore?

Adversity is a part of everyone's lives and professions, so resilience—the capacity to keep going after your goals in the face of difficulty—is a crucial problem for companies. We all suffer personal hardships, such as the everyday pressures of juggling our obligations at home and at work, the loss of a loved one, or social stressors like a pandemic or a rise in broadcast racist violence. Resilience in the face of these difficulties is crucial.

However, present organisational efforts to strengthen employee resilience are usually unsuccessful. There are legitimate worries about resilience turning into an exploitative, stigmatising, and overvalued phenomenon. The majority of employee resilience training initiatives have had rather tiny and transient results. Resilience is frequently viewed as "a doubling down on classic bootstrap thinking, where your success or failure comes down to your character," according to former New York Times Magazine writer Parul Sehgal. In light of the fact that resilience is both crucial and problematic, how can companies increase their efforts to promote it while being aware of its drawbacks? This includes both targeted interventions and standing policies like paid leave, well-being resources, and physical accommodations. I advise recognising hazards, avoiding them, and responding to three reflection queries.

Consider resilience as a condition that any employee may achieve rather than a personality attribute. To achieve this, settings that proactively promote resilience must be fostered.

- Does your organisation's culture support employees speaking out and utilising resources to address their needs, suggestions, and concerns?

- Do your organisation's leave, accommodation, and benefit policies allow employees to respond to obstacles in a suitable manner?

Even if certain obstacles may come as a surprise, organisations should nonetheless prepare for them. Employees might not be able to foresee a miscarriage, sexual harassment, or a period of declining mental health, but your organisation can develop rules to address such potential events in advance.

This viewpoint also emphasises the fact that measures to promote resilience should not take the place of systematic efforts to eliminate inequality. For instance, it is improper to tell black employees to "be more resilient" in the face of racism and discrimination without addressing the underlying reasons why such resilience is required in the first place. Organisations might instead concentrate on developing an inclusive culture and specialised equity-supporting policies.

You must be aware that two things might happen at once if you want to establish true resilience in your organisation: While corporations provide proactive tools and implement measures that serve to safeguard employees, individuals may construct a reservoir of resources, such as optimism, energy, and established social support networks, to draw from to help them be resilient. Employee resiliency cannot take the place of organisational development and support. Employers stigmatise their employees when they face hardship.

Negative emotions frequently surface while a person is coping with a difficult situation, even if pleasant emotions can foster resilience. This is normal in the human experience; in fact, people may still be resilient even while they are experiencing unpleasant emotions, provided they don't become pathologically strong or persistent. But far too frequently, when someone feels or expresses irritation, worry, or overload at work, they are ostracised. As a consequence, since they worry about being criticised, employees might not ask for help. The lack of unpleasant emotions during difficult circumstances should not be equated with resilience in organisational resilience initiatives. In actuality, such associations could be unreal and unhelpful.

Principles of mindfulness, such as accepting feelings without judgement, have established advantages, such as bettering both physical and emotional health. Frustration after an unwelcome change or feeling overburdened while juggling job and care obligations are not examples of "non-resilience." While continuing to work toward their objectives, employees are capable of experiencing complicated emotional situations. Instead of attempting to suppress unfavourable emotions, organisations may use them as indicators to determine whether internal issues need to be resolved and the best ways to help employees.

Once you are aware of hazards and their prevalence within your team or organisation, you can start to reevaluate how you can support people in developing resilience. Can the adversity be lessened or eliminated? It's crucial to assess if the business can deal with the adversity before selecting how to handle employee resilience.

If the answer to this question is "no," it seems reasonable to concentrate your efforts on educating and encouraging employees members‘ resilience-building practices. For instance, while the main reason for a worker's unanticipated caregiving responsibilities cannot be fixed, paid time off, flexible work policies, and supportive supervisors are organisational tools that might contribute to boosting resilience. Delivering employees specialised support when required, such as offering training to assist an employee in navigating a difficult new task, may be necessary to foster an atmosphere that promotes resilience.

If the answer to this question is "yes"—as in the case of abusive work cultures, unrealistic employee task loads, or pay inequity—organisations should instead concentrate on strategies to reduce employees' need for resilience in such cases. Effective support requires asking employees what they are struggling with and what they need to overcome the adversity. Potential organisational solutions to the issue of a heavy workload include changing job loads, adding employees, or giving higher compensation in return for larger workloads. One economical and successful technique to determine the effects of adversity is to seek employee feedback through surveys and focus groups. This allows for tailored answers and improves employees' perceptions of being heard.

What role can you play in encouraging employee resilience?

The resilience of employees can and should be actively supported by leaders. Although there is a propensity to romanticise leadership, imputing to these people sole responsibility for both positive and negative outcomes, it is true that leaders have a significant impact on organisational culture and norms and are crucial in fostering a culture of shared resilience responsibility. Leaders should consider the following in order to respond to this question:

The tools they have available to support employee resilience. These can include providing paid counselling services, paid time off, establishing employee resource groups and incorporating their recommendations, as well as fostering an environment at work where employees members can express their needs and concerns without fear of punishment.

Through the actions they reward, they communicate what they value and want their subordinates to prioritise. This entails not just encouraging certain actions, like asking for help, but also creating a culture that values making errors and growing from them. Building a culture that values employee input and learning strengthens resiliency. The kinds of accommodations they provide, which show that they are aware that hardship may affect how much work employees can produce, show that they are aware that employees are people, not machines. Respecting employees' humanity by modifying individual or team expectations in response to a setback fosters an atmosphere where resilience is feasible.

The room they create for a variety of employee feelings. Avoid, in particular, imposing the standard that individuals should only feel good through adversity or, even worse, that they should feel nothing at all when faced with a serious problem. Employees are forced to use internal resources to control impressions instead of using them to meet the task at hand when they are implicitly or explicitly asked to seem unaffected in a challenging scenario. Recognising the humanity of employees includes promoting healthy emotional expression as well.

Despite its drawbacks, businesses should keep promoting resilience among their employees members. All occupations involve tasks that are vulnerable to stresses; hence, resilience is required at all occupational stages, levels, and types. The advantages of resilience for our personal and professional lives make initiatives to improve resilience more successful than giving up on it completely. Knowing that they can, at least in part, regulate their responses to trying circumstances empowers employees. However, it's also critical to see the bigger picture, which takes into account the power and influence that leaders and organisations have on the experiences and results of employee resilience. A lack of methods and support for people confronting hardship might result from the elimination of resilience initiatives. Only when the burden of resilience is shared can attempts at resilience be effective and long-lasting.

Executives are under a lot of internal and external pressure to succeed. They are always struggling to make sense of their shifting environments and to decide what is best for themselves, their teams, and their organisation. The effective tactics ambitious executives require to become genuine leaders in the twenty-first century are provided by Executive Advantage. It clarifies the challenges businesses confront, particularly in the face of strong expansion or, alternatively, recession and downsising.

What if you had the ability to see things happening in your organisation and in your personal relationships that others weren't aware of? And what if you were able to consider what you saw from a distinct, novel perspective—one that gave you insights that enabled you to comprehend ordinarily perplexing circumstances in great detail? What if you had the ability to see things happening in your organisation and in your personal relationships that others weren't aware of? And what if you were able to consider what you saw from a distinct, novel perspective—one that gave you insights that enabled you to comprehend ordinarily perplexing circumstances in great detail?

Resilient leaders aren't afraid of failure.

As an organisation grows, it is inevitable that it will face uncertainty. Leaders who can assist employees through difficult periods and learn to solve recurring issues may have a significant influence on the process. That is why resilient leadership is critical. resilient leadership is a management philosophy that aims to help businesses embrace change and uncertainty rather than merely handle them. This allows businesses to successfully adjust while maintaining their core principles and strengths. Change has taken on a three-dimensional form. It's all-encompassing, never-ending, and rapidly expanding. Leaders can no longer operate in a vacuum, making decisions and taking actions from the "helm" of a organisation. Leaders must adapt in order for organisations to succeed in today's atmosphere. The "leader-as-hero" style is no longer effective, and the alternative represents a transition toward more intelligent, collaborative leadership. resilient leadership is the term for this. In comparison to contemporary paradigms, it radiates more honesty, humility, and vulnerability.

"Leadership is lifting a person's vision to high sights, the raising of a person's performance to a higher standard, the building of a personality beyond its normal limitations."

—Peter Drucker

Leaders with an resilient style are performance-driven, self-aware, and have a high level of emotional intelligence. They delegate the appropriate responsibilities to the appropriate individuals and give resources for professional growth. While they do take decisive action, they almost never do it in a reactionary manner without taking into account all possible consequences. Because they establish dynamic teams that welcome change and channel anxiety into positive outcomes, resilient leaders get better results. When your organisation is confronted with a technological transformation, a new client preference, or a new marketing dynamic such as the current economy, you must awaken the leader inside you to lead others through these changes. When your workload, team members, clients, and resources change on a regular basis, your leadership and management style must adapt as well.

Although the characteristic approach has been around for decades, there has been a rising focus on abilities that are particularly significant for resilient leadership in recent years. These abilities include the capacity to comprehend the leadership position and the flexibility to modify methods or actions in response to changing circumstances. Although evidence for the effects of certain talents on effective leadership is still scarce, the amount of research has increased in recent years. A study in which measurements of leadership abilities and personality are connected with markers of leadership effectiveness and, in some cases, with leadership behavior is the most common research strategy.

J.K. Rowling's inspiring story of success unless you've been living under a rock, you've heard of the Harry Potter series. However, the author is rather certain that most of you haven't heard of J.K. Rowling. If you're wondering who she is, she's the lady behind the world's most successful bestseller series. This remarkable woman is motivating and extraordinary in every way. Rowling's triumph is one of the most exhilarating, but it wasn't always smooth sailing. Few people know what happened to her before she became famous. J.K. Rowling's success story It is stated that true success follows a series of setbacks. This is precisely what happened to Rowling. Her personal life was in disarray, making each day difficult for her.

Not to mention that her novel was made into a film series, making it a billion-dollar franchise. Are there any takeaways for you all? J.K. Rowling's most important lesson is to keep trying, believing, and acting on your dreams. Whether it's to become a great business or to publish a novel, there's something for everyone.

Resilient leadership theory helps professionals anticipate and identify the fundamental causes of problems and discover long-term solutions. This necessitates leaders being more than merely commanding officers. Instead, they must be receptive to input, ready for change, and willing to reverse direction if required.

Steve Jobs, Elon Musk, Mark Zuckerberg, and Oprah Winfrey are just a few examples of outstanding men and women who became phenomenally wealthy by taking chances and working smart. Elon Musk is the ultimate risk-taker and entrepreneur. Elon Musk is one of the few entrepreneurs who have never played it safe. He's been taking chances since the beginning. Some people were unsuccessful, while others were fortunate enough to win the lottery. To take on eBay, he joined with a rival and renamed the new business PayPal, which completely transformed the world of electronic payments. Musk was the largest stakeholder and walked away with $180 million when eBay purchased PayPal for $1.5 billion shortly after.

It's critical to use resilient leadership to overcome problems. It's critical to understand the distinction between a technical and an resilient problem while using resilient leadership to overcome obstacles. A single-time solution can solve a technological problem completely. resilient difficulties are time-consuming and may necessitate organisational culture adjustments. They frequently occur during periods of expansion or transition, and they entail everyone in the organisation changing their long-term plans. Resilient leadership's proactive character necessitates the recognition that some of the organisation's existing business processes are unproductive. Resilient leaders have a set of characteristics that they constantly display. Any person in the organisation may be a leader under an resilient leadership model, and these attributes can be cultivated over time. Every resilient leader should have the following characteristics:

- The ability to link organisational change to the primary values, abilities, and dreams of the stakeholders involved.
- The ability to create an environment that embraces diversity of viewpoints and uses such collective knowledge to benefit the organisation.
- The resilient leader recognises that change is a difficult process. As a result, he or she can anticipate and counteract any hesitant conduct on the part of colleagues.
- An knowledge that large-scale change is a slow process that needs perseverance and the fortitude to face the pressure that comes with it.
- Being proactive in seeking out possibilities and devoting the resources necessary to pursue them. Admitting when they've made a mistake and altering or discarding ineffective techniques.
- Being willing to try new things and take risks. Employees like and are encouraged to innovate.

- Resilient leadership isn't about having a lot of power. It's about developing a feeling of organisational accountability in the whole workforce. Leadership is a shared responsibility. Leadership cannot always be the responsibility of one person in a world of constant and volatile change.
- Resilient leaders develop employee who can foresee what will happen, prepare for it, adjust to it, recover from setbacks, and keep going even when things are difficult.
- Resilient leaders instill a feeling of common purpose in their teams and govern by influence rather than by command and control.
- Resilient leadership necessitates new talents and competences, such as spirit, guts, heart, and mind. It takes guts to present your complete self to the conversation.
- Resilient leaders encourage teams to generate outcomes by empowering people, and they give lots of praise and celebration for the team's achievement. They share the limelight with the squad and ensure that they get lots of favorable press for their work.
- Resilient leaders are open to change and embrace it. It's the truth for them. They form dynamic teams that welcome change and use cooperation and communication to transform any uncertainty into great outcomes.
- Resilient leaders make sure their employees are knowledgeable about the organisation's strategy and the context in which they operate, and then they step aside. Rather than checking in on their teammates, they check in. They also provide employees the freedom to work through concerns and solve problems.

- The resilient leader must demonstrate resilience on a daily basis so that the capacity to handle adversity, remain cheerful and hopeful, and respond calmly to difficult events pervades the business.
- Resilient leaders have a set of characteristics that they constantly display. Any person in the organisation may be a leader under an resilient leadership model, and these attributes can be cultivated over time.
- Resilient leaders connect long-term corporate objectives to systematic transformation.Action is conducted with the goal of achieving a certain outcome in mind.
- Resilient leaders foster a progressive and open-minded work environment. Errors are recognised as a necessary part of the process.
- Resilient leaders recognize and embrace adversity. They get their team members ready to solve problems. resilient leaders recognise that finding a long-term solution may take a few tries.
- Resilient leaders understand that change takes time and are willing to put in the time required to build a better organisation.
- Resilient leaders are proactive in their approach. They detect problems and spend whatever resources are required to remedy them ahead of time.
- Resilient leaders state their intentions openly and then let the participants play the game. The participants will either win or lose the game in the end.
- Resilient leaders value relationships as much as they value money. This knowledge aids them in ensuring that organisational members and other stakeholders are on board with any long-term changes.

- Emotional intelligence is a trait shared by resilient leaders. As a result, they can immediately determine how an employee feels about a certain circumstance. In this part of the resilient leadership paradigm, the affiliate leadership style might be effective. Once the leader understands the emotions at play, he or she can give the appropriate support so that this individual may continue to perform at their best. This, of course, necessitates a great deal of empathy on the part of the leader.
- Resilient leadership may be summarised using four basic principles: dispersed leadership, appropriate talent mix, transparent character, and development. When it comes to dispersed leadership, the leader assigns duties to members of the team.
- Resilient leaders are at ease with the unknown.They understand that not having a quick solution to an issue is an important element of the positive transformation process.
- Resilient leaders enjoy experimenting with new ideas and solving problems.They are ready to evaluate their work and make adjustments as needed. They recognize that handling nebulous and difficult topics necessitates trial and error.

Flexible or resilient leadership entails altering behavior in response to changing circumstances. Leaders who can effectively evaluate a situation and adjust their conduct accordingly have been referred to by a number of words. Flexible, resilient, agile, and versatile are examples of these adjectives. There is still a lot of misunderstanding in management and leadership literature regarding what flexible leadership is and how to evaluate it. Resiliente leadership may occur in a variety of situations, which adds to the uncertainty. For example, when situations change for a leader, flexibility is essential, as is flexibility when transferring from one sort of leadership role to another with different duties and tasks.

Behavioral flexibility and resiliency may be characterised and quantified in a variety of ways, with the signs varying depending on the circumstance. The degree to which a leader employs a range of diverse behaviors is one sign. To be resilient, however, the chosen behaviors must be appropriate for the conditions in which they are utilised. As a result, the extent to which a leader's conduct varies in ways that are acceptable for different tasks and subordinates is a stronger predictor of flexibility. In a normal day or week, most leaders are responsible for a variety of duties, and it is sometimes required to move swiftly from one sort of work to another. Different jobs typically necessitate different leadership styles.

Furthermore, because subordinates differ in terms of experience, talents, beliefs, and requirements, a leader's conduct with various individuals should vary. For subordinates with good talents and a strong dedication to work objectives, for example, increased delegation is suitable. When a subordinate's talents and motivations vary over time, flexibility is also essential. Using the same scenario, greater delegation will be acceptable as a subordinate acquires experience and confidence.

It is never a good idea to give up. Agree?

Walt Disney didn't have an easy life. Because quitting was never an option for Walt Disney, a guy of action, determination, aspirations, and passion, he altered the world of entertainment and animation. Do you know that Walt Disney was once fired from a newspaper for being too creative? His first animation organisation, however, was a flop. His theme park concept was turned down. His first several animated flicks failed miserably. If he had been going through a bad patch, Walt would have become one of those homeless men yelling about his failure. He didn't give up, though. Now you're all talking about his success. His animation organisation became the most well-known in the world, and Disney Land and Disney World are two of the most popular and profitable theme parks in the world.

Many successful people have gone through the same thing, and you're talking about them now. So reconsider! What do you do when you're on the verge of giving up? Are you afraid of taking risks? Learn how to be a great performer. You must take chances regardless of whether you are a risk taker or not. To be honest, you may have taken a few chances to get to where you are now, and you will continue to do so in the future. Then why not go all-in and do things that terrify the very daylights out of us? What makes you fearful of taking risks? Risk is defined as the possibility of losing anything significant, such as money, a job, one's health, a relationship, or anything else that is precious or dear to you.

The capacity to grasp the leadership situation, including political processes and social interactions, as well as the ability to pick an acceptable reaction and alter one's conduct in response to changing situations, is referred to as social intelligence. Empathy, self-awareness, and the capacity to control one's own emotions are all examples of emotional intelligence. Empathy for others' sentiments is critical when deciding how to influence and motivate them. The capacity to recognise your own ideals, intentions, and effectiveness in influencing others is referred to as self-awareness. Self-control of emotions entails the capacity to avoid mood swings and emotional reactions that obstruct problem solutions, such as panic during a crisis.

One of the big five personality qualities is openness to learning and new ideas, which is critical for leaders who must adapt to changing circumstances. This characteristic involves the capacity to take feedback regarding the influence of your actions on others. A person who depends on habitual patterns of conduct while ignoring negative feedback or fresh ideas is unlikely to be resilient and flexible. Success in higher-level employment is predicted by the capacity to learn from experience. Feedback from many sources (e.g., subordinates, peers, employers, clients) may help a leader become more aware of key qualities, abilities, and behaviors, and coaching is vital for leaders who must adapt to changing situations.

Resilient leadership, as I perceive, poses a number of difficulties. Experimenting, learning new information, and making multiple modifications throughout your organisation are all part of this leadership paradigm. You will only be able to maintain the changes and prosper if you modify your mindset and adjust your policies. Changing people's attitudes, beliefs, and perceptions, on the other hand, is frequently more difficult than flossing a cat's teeth.

Making adjustments necessitates a degree of disloyalty to your past. If you wish to execute a new marketing strategy, for example, you must first accept that your existing marketing methods are unsuccessful. Most top executives are hesitant to abandon long-standing rules that helped their organisations get off the ground. Sticking to old habits, on the other hand, might prevent you from reaping the benefits of new tactics. Another issue with resilient leadership is that it creates an environment conducive to various types of opposition. This might be from your employees or other stakeholders in the organisation. Stakeholder Any individual, group, or entity with an interest in an organisation and the effects of its activities is referred to as a stakeholder in business.

Marginalising, distracting, and assaulting are the most prevalent techniques used to stymie resilient change. If you see any of these behaviors, it's likely that your employees are resisting the new policy you're attempting to impose. The refusal of leaders to listen to other people's perspectives is perhaps the biggest obstacle posed by resilient leadership. resilient leadership, as previously said, is more about cooperation than it is about power. resilient leaders, in principle, should be open to listening to and modifying suggestions made by coemployees or clients.

In actuality, only a small number of leaders are prepared to listen to others who disagree with them. What such leaders fail to realise is that listening does not always imply forsaking one's own objectives. It simply implies that you have a better understanding of your employees' requirements. As a result, you'll be able to work more efficiently to implement modifications. Although resilient leadership demands a significant amount of work, it pays off handsomely. resilient businesses, according to trustworthy statistics, reap enormous financial and operational benefits. Even during moments of turbulence, they are able to withstand storms and surge to the top.

Examining the issue to determine which obstacles are technical and which are resilient Leaders must manage emotionally charged circumstances based on opposing values, beliefs, and loyalties while scoping. Experts and traditional problem-solving approaches have repeatedly attempted but failed to address the problem, which is a telltale indicator of resilient difficulties.

Diagnose the environment in order to identify and comprehend people, processes, and technological systems and subsystems that maintain the status quo and the factions that profit from and protect the status quo. This involves learning about cultural norms, traditions, and rituals in a certain setting. The environment must be diagnosed before the adaptation challenge can be diagnosed. Diagnoses come before cures, just as they do in medicine.

The expert in resilient leadership, that leaders who understand and support flexibility have a distinct perspective on their employees. They encourage everyone in the organisation to take on a leadership position. resilient leaders aim to create a working culture where informal leaders throughout the business are innovating and pushing change from the bottom up, rather than the conventional position where the leader takes the choices and they are pushed down from the top. However, encouraging employees at all levels to take responsibility rather than expecting to be given solutions and told what to do may be a significant cultural adjustment for many businesses.

This unique, world-class, cutting-edge approach to how a organisation operates does not arise by chance. According to me , an organisation's senior leadership should ask, "What are our values and how do we live them?" "How do they appear at different levels of the organisation?" Then there should be open and honest discussions with middle management, as well as input from them. Employees must also be included when you explain this new way of thinking and determine whether they are interested in taking on a larger role. This is in stark contrast to what can occur, for instance, at a yearly performance review, while assessing someone's progress. That discussion might be about a certain degree, course, or goal that someone is pursuing.

It's a more comprehensive view of each individual in resilient leadership than just their job description. "These are the strengths I see in you, and here's how I'd want to leverage them so you can shine here," you say to the individual. Here are the flaws you see and to help you in those areas, I would want to place you in a safe atmosphere where you can work on them and see if you can get better at them with a little practice. You are better prepared for the difficulties and changes ahead when you draw on your particular talents, abilities, and expertise. Employees at all levels are happy because they have the opportunity to advance, lead, and shine. In essence, an resilient leader recognises and capitalises on an employee's individuality. Identifying a person's flaws and assisting them in improving them, or accepting that not everyone is competent at everything.

As a result, resilient leadership nearly always requires you to analyse, manage, distribute, and provide context for losses in order to move people to a new location. Answering concerns concerning resilient change and the losses it entails is challenging in any case because it necessitates difficult decisions, trade-offs, and the uncertainty of continual experimental trial and error. That is a difficult job not only because it is academically challenging, but also because it tests people and organisations' commitment to connections, competence, and identity. It necessitates a change in the tales they've told themselves and the rest of the world about what they believe in, stand for, and represent.

Resilient leadership is the discipline of organising individuals to face and overcome difficult circumstances. The notion that you need to reform organisations because they are "dysfunctional" is a misconception. In actuality, human systems work the way they do because the people who live in them want them to. When you realise this, you'll change the way you approach the situation. If you realise that a seemingly dysfunctional organisation is actually operating for many of its members, then you'll use a variety of strategies and approaches. Rather than trying to persuade people that your image of the organisation is correct, you'll learn to focus on how to motivate and support them through a hazardous and terrifying transformation.

Resilient leaders must be able to self-manage in the face of uncertainty, as well as assist others in dealing with their own discomfort. When you ask people and organisations challenging questions and ask them to be accountable for matters that are outside the scope of their professions, they feel disequilibrium. The temperature of a productive disequilibrium is continually managed by an resilient leader. Only by staying in this productive zone are teams and organisations able to deal with complex adaptation difficulties.

Resilient leaders and their teams become more resilient as a result of their resiliency. They get stronger as a result of their blunders. Leaders who keep going and endure in the face of adversity attain success. When they stop trying, they call it "failure." resilient leaders allow everyone to make mistakes. It will re-energise a company.

"I have not failed," Thomas Edison is reported as saying. I've come up with 10,000 methods that won't work. "

Development of resilient leadership a new leadership development framework is required. One that can be given at scale and creates resilient leaders at all levels, sooner in their careers and in the flow of their work. The new model stresses learning in the context of the organisation's business conditions, processes, and objectives, as well as quick implementation of what has been learned. Starting with helping leaders understand the business, including its goals, mission, and goods and services, there are multiple activities and numerous keys to producing resilient leaders.

Resilient ability will continue to determine who emerges on top and who goes away in 2022. HR executives can assist corporate leaders in evaluating their default habits and embracing their ability to adjust. The epidemic shook up the corporate world, especially in terms of how people see leadership, delegation, performance management, and trust. It also prompted concerns regarding remote work productivity, procedures that obstruct existing processes, new health and safety-related job standards, and how to benefit from new production and delivery methods. The ability of businesses to respond to these issues is strongly tied to their executives' ability to adapt.

Take a step back and consider the overall difficulty of the situation. To gain perspective and understand the larger picture, an resilient leader must switch between being an observer and being a participant. Assess the situation to determine whether the challenge is technical or resilient in nature. Resilient difficulties are complicated, fluid, and alter with conditions, whereas technical challenges may be handled by an expert's expertise. If the problem is resilient, the leader should collaborate with stakeholders to overcome it using calculative steps. Leaders must always provide coherence to a continuous improvement process by buffering it from—or linking it to—other imperatives that exist in a district at any given time if it is to thrive. Leaders will encounter conflicting expectations without any buffering or bridging, making it impossible to produce anything cohesive.

Resilient leaders aren't afraid of failure. You pay close attention to the effort required to navigate the resilient difficulty. Many people will try to resist change since it forces them to labor outside of their comfort zone. Ignoring the difficulty, blaming others, or diverting one's efforts are all examples of avoidance behaviors. Instead of avoiding the problem, an resilient leader assists stakeholders in confronting it head-on. When negotiating the resilient hurdles connected with school reform initiatives, it's crucial to remember that these resilient leadership typically occur concurrently and interdependently.

Resilient leaders create environments that encourage experimentation, learning, and reflection on both success and failure. Failure is viewed as a learning opportunity by resilient leaders, and experimentation is praised even if the desired objective is not reached. The important thing is to keep going ahead. It's critical to figure out why something failed quickly and then move on. If they aren't making errors, the resilient leader believes they aren't working hard enough.

Successful organisations that accept failure are Netflix, Amazon, and Coca-Cola. You can't learn unless you fail, and you can't achieve until you face obstacles. Traditional leadership training methods appear to take individuals as they are and turn them into leaders by talking to them about leadership concepts and abilities. There is some self-exploration, but your impression is that the courses move on to the notion of leadership relatively rapidly, with less emphasis on self-exploration as a leader. However, in my opinion, who you are is the most important component in defining the type of leader you will be. Your training as integrated coaches supports this viewpoint. You strive to figure out who you are and what it entails for your leadership style and decisions. When you engage with your executive customers to help them develop their businesses.

A leader should ask, "What opposing values and power conflicts exist in this scenario, and how will I consider the complete context in assisting others in navigating the difficulty at hand?"

Now is the moment for businesses to build leaders who can adjust themselves and their organisations to deal with disruptions while doing their daily tasks. The ability of businesses to adjust to changing circumstances is critical. Disruptions can be viewed as a danger, which requires resistance, or as an opportunity, which requires adaptation. Resilient organisations, according to Deloitte, will succeed. To become an resilient company, large-scale global enterprises must make a fundamental shift in operating and management philosophy that allows them to function with a start-up mindset and drive current people practices that enable enterprise agility through an empowered network of teams. Leaders must leave their comfort zones and take on resilient problems with no obvious answers in order to prepare for the future. Hierarchies must play a supporting role in enabling a constantly evolving network of teams. These groups require resilient leaders.

Leaders who are resilient, the way people live, work, and conduct business will continue to be shaped and reshaped by long-term upheaval and change. Resilient organisations must look beyond incremental development and address current practices‘ flaws on a regular basis. Resilient leaders need to climb up on the roof from time to time to observe what’s coming over the horizon. When they detect the potential for disruption, they must move rapidly to plan responses in concert with other leaders.

Leaders must analyse their behaviors and how they effect their companies as part of resilient leadership training. HR can ensure that leaders learn from the past, adapt to the present, and prepare for the future by effectively transforming and demonstrating resilient capacity. CEOs are afraid that their leaders will be unprepared to deal with expected challenges. They also desire greater results from their leadership development efforts. That entails creating resilient leadership skills and providing them at an organisational level for the chief learning officer and learning and development professionals. There are two barriers preventing businesses from responding to new circumstances. First, hierarchical arrangements, for starters, stifle team effectiveness by reducing decision-making and communication. Second, the majority of team leaders are actually process managers who are at ease in their technical operations zone but uncomfortable when there are disturbances. They attempt to apply operational abilities to resilient obstacles, but instead of generating fresh solutions, they resort to patching problems.

Change is unavoidable. Be tenacious. Agree?

An resilient leader isn’t surprised by change. Instead, this leader has put in place procedures and tactics to deal with problems as they emerge. When an resilient leader is present, at least one backup plan is always easily available.

You are living in an era of both peril and opportunity. To merely live, individuals, businesses, communities, and countries must constantly adapt to new circumstances. People in all sectors are being called upon to lead with the confidence and skill to question the status quo, deploy themselves with agility, and organise others to go into the unknown because they want more and want to prosper even in continuously shifting and often risky conditions. Resilient leaders know how to invent alternate uses of things to promote their vision, just as core and effective leaders know how to identify what should and shouldn't work. Core leadership, equals book smarts, successful leadership equals street smarts, and resilient leadership means inventiveness. To put it another way, core leaders are recognised for their competency, successful leaders for their expertise, and resilient leaders for their visions with flexible paths. The greater the level of uncertainty, the more untrainable leadership development is infused. Because of the speed at which change occurs, companies must learn more quickly, more thoroughly, and more extensively than ever before. Focusing solely on guiding the moment and directing the future is no longer sufficient. Rather, every activity, strategy, job, and communication should be part of a continuous cycle of improvement and iteration.

Because of the epidemic, the way you work has changed, and leaders must adapt accordingly. While some organisations have chosen to remain with remote work, others have chosen a hybrid strategy that includes some in-office time. The shift in the work model has posed a challenge to hybrid leadership. As a result, leaders will need a new set of abilities to keep their employees engaged and productive in the new hybrid workplace. New management issues have arisen as a result of the hybrid work approach. Improved leadership abilities that can adapt to changing work conditions are required by the new hybrid model. Upskilling has become more important for better leadership. In a hybrid culture, leaders must continually develop, learn, and unlearn. Leaders should draw on prior experiences to develop the leadership abilities necessary in a hybrid work environment, even if it has been a learning process for everyone. This may be accomplished through leadership development programs that are specifically geared to promoting strong leadership that is necessary for enhancing workplace culture. Build trust in the workplace. In this climate, managers demand more resilient leadership management, which can be done through a variety of leadership development programs that will assist the organisation in going to the next level.

"Notwithstanding the challenging societal circumstances at this moment presented by the Omicron surge, CEOs remain optimistic about the business environment and see strong growth opportunities over the next year."— Joe Ucuzoglu, Chief Executive Officer, Deloitte US

A new normal appears to be setting in whereby business leaders simply expect new challenges to arise continuously, and are confident they can manage through them to achieve positive business results while making a real difference in society. Leadership is the responsibility of everyone, and it is assumed by the individual who is best positioned to make a decision or take action. Allowing leadership to be distributed is at the heart of adaptive leadership. Resilient leaders develop employees who can foresee what will happen, prepare for it, adjust to it, recover from setbacks, and keep going even when things are difficult. The resilient leader must demonstrate resilience on a daily basis so that the capacity to handle adversity, remain cheerful and hopeful, and respond calmly to difficult events pervades the business. Resilient leaders instill a feeling of common purpose in their teams and govern by influence rather than by command and control. Leadership must be resilient in the face of volatile, uncertain, complex, and ambiguous change. Resilient leaders must be able to determine when to enter the conflict and when to exit and observe from the sidelines.

As a leader, you must help people realise how what they gain is crucial to their basic beliefs and how the change will aid in the evolution of their traditions rather than depreciate them. Resilient leaders have a deep awareness of each employee's strengths and weaknesses, and they manage them appropriately. Resilient leaders have a high level of flexibility, i.e., the capacity to seamlessly go from traditional to adaptive leadership styles. Resilient leaders are driven to achieve excellent results and to infuse their enthusiasm and fire into their teams. Because they expect plans to alter, adaptive leaders always have contingency plans in place. Resilient leaders use quick, fluid communication to keep everyone on the same page. They also encourage team participation, which inevitably leads to fewer mistakes and higher quality work. It builds trust and provides psychological stability for the people it leads, allowing them to continue to learn, grow, and contribute to a shared future. Resilient leadership recognises that the whole is more than the sum of its parts in the proper Aristotelian sense. That the organisation as a whole will perform better when each employee feels safe, confident, and trusted by their leadership. Resilient leadership, when done well, instills togetherness, ambition, and resilience in a team.

Resilient leadership is to find a middle ground where the business, external stakeholders, and rivals can all benefit from the solutions you provide. This may seem counterintuitive if you're used to working simply as a competitor, but if you and your competitors can support each other, it'll be well worth your time and money. Another fundamental element of resilient leadership is to promote and nurture an honest culture. Resilient executives are well-versed in the finest policies that can be implemented to help the organisation. They can also efficiently execute such rules in a way that people accept them. Every employee feels appreciated and respected because their thoughts and ideas are heard and considered. As more new ideas are presented, this has a ripple effect across the business. This encourages more buy-in, which is necessary for the solution's effective implementation. Resilient leadership should provide their employees with the most up-to-date technologies to increase efficiency and production while reducing time and effort spent on various activities.

Resilient leaders use quick, fluid communication to keep everyone on the same page. They also encourage team participation, which inevitably leads to fewer mistakes and higher quality work. Resilient leaders have productive and friendly relationships with their coworkers. Resilient leaders and their teams routinely look outside the box rather than sticking to tried-and-true techniques. Teams and organisations must evaluate their performance on a regular basis, identifying strong and weak areas and making modifications to improve results. Continuous learning and progress are the names of the game on other planets.

Resilient leadership is to find a middle ground where the business, external stakeholders, and rivals can all benefit from the solutions you provide. This may seem counterintuitive if you're used to working simply as a competitor, but if you and your competitors can support each other, it'll be well worth your time and money. They will view losing a game as a learning experience, and the squad will regroup and prepare for the next game. They will be able to empathise with others and put themselves in their position to comprehend their point of view. Players are encouraged to take responsibility and make decisions.

Resilient leaders are open to change and embrace it. It's the truth for them. They form dynamic teams that welcome change and use cooperation and communication to transform any uncertainty into great outcomes. Resilient leaders state their intentions openly and then let the participants play the game. The participants will either win or lose the game in the end. Resilient leadership isn't about having a lot of power. It's about developing a feeling of organisational accountability in the whole workforce. Learning is impossible without some risk and failure. While conventional leaders may seek for green lights on the dashboard progress report, resilient leaders encourage individuals to be open about where they've pushed themselves and where they may be struggling—the truth. Resilient leaders encourage teams to generate outcomes by empowering people, and they give lots of praise and celebration for the team's achievement. They share the limelight with the squad and ensure that they get lots of favorable press for their work.

In order to make positive changes happen, senior leaders must first be open to suggestions from employees at all levels. Mid-level supervisors must coach employees on how to convey ideas and information in a compelling manner. Everyone must believe they are capable of bringing about change. Everyone must feel comfortable discussing or disagreeing about what is going on. At every stage of the game, employees must know how to be informal leaders. Naturally, in a dysfunctional workplace, an intimidating individual or someone who dominates the discourse might obstruct this. The adaptive leader is once again called upon to teach and assist all employees in developing the skills necessary to deal with dysfunctionality in an emotionally intelligent and caring manner. By doing so, he or she is equipping workers with the communication tools they need to get beyond these disruptive situations, as well as ensuring that all viewpoints are valuable to the organisation and that all voices count, even those who aren't conscious of their impact.

Many changes entail adaptation issues that require people to develop new skills. In corporate and community transformation attempts, this is frequently disregarded. People must adapt to address challenges in order for the shift to be effective. Adapt or change is required of both leaders and individuals. Individuals must develop their own capacity to solve issues and capitalise on opportunities. Many of your greater societal crises, such as climate change, do not have a technology solution to transition from individual to systemic challenges. You need people to modify what they do until there is a technological answer, and you need to address the bigger adaptive issues involved in making these adjustments, which include, among other things, value systems and identity. Leaders must mobilize their followers to modify existing habits and build new ones. Resilient leaders keep their heritage alive by refining or evolving it. If this growth hurts relationships , the ties must be renegotiated as part of the transformation process. Deeply held beliefs and identities may be impacted by these shifts. If these values and identities are thoroughly and compassionately addressed, change may strengthen rather than weaken the foundation on which the organisation or community was created.In the transition process, each team member plays an important role.

Workplaces and settings are always changing. Because your workload, team members, clients, and resources are always changing, your leadership and management style must change as well. Allowing your team to have fun at work is one way to guarantee that they adjust to the shift and continually offer the ideas that matter. Allow them to laugh out loud during cooperation calls to lighten the tone. Alternatively, pick an alternative venue for brainstorming, such as an office park or a organisation lunch. Also, be open to all ideas rather than dismissing them as "dumb." Remember that a funny or "dumb" concept that makes it to a brainstorming session might transform into a fantastic out-of-the-box idea with more discussion. Even when faced with uncertainty, leaders who challenge current conventions, ask questions, and arrange dispute resolution assist the organisation in overcoming any challenge and emerging victorious.

Resilient leaders have productive and friendly relationships with their coworkers. Resilient leaders and their teams routinely look outside the box rather than sticking to tried-and-true techniques. Resilient leadership necessitates a high level of self-awareness on the part of the leaders, as well as an understanding of how their verbal and non-verbal communication affects the team. Making errors is a natural part of the process. Nobody can accomplish everything perfectly the first time. Accepting mistakes, learning from them, and making course changes are all part of adaptive learning. Teams and organisations must evaluate their performance on a regular basis, identifying strong and weak areas and making modifications to improve results. Continuous learning and progress are the names of the game on other planets.

A successful, resilient leader recognises this and places team members in locations that allow their individual abilities to flourish. They also give resources to help build and maintain these strengths. An resilient leader does not reward a team member for their pleasant working relationship. This leader, on the other hand, awards prizes depending on performance. In the transition process, each team member plays an important role. A successful, resilient leader recognises this and places team members in locations that allow their individual abilities to flourish. They also give resources to help build and maintain these strengths. It's not about keeping track of the number of hours or work performed in a day; it's about whether this team member can meet the deadline. Resilient leadership has certain pacesetting streaks as a result of this. Furthermore, the incentives are not necessarily monetary. They range from providing employees with paid time off to year-long fellowships that help them advance professionally. In essence, rewards are also handled in an adaptive manner.

Leadership is a shared responsibility. Leadership cannot always be the responsibility of one person in a world of constant and volatile change. Of course, teams must be capable in order to be effective in solving their own problems. Employees benefit from both formal and embedded learning opportunities, such as work shadowing and job rotation, provided by great agile leaders. Resilient leaders don't wait for a slowdown to grow their people—they know those are rare—instead, they use busy moments to stretch and challenge team members to contribute in new ways and through new responsibilities that stretch and challenge them. Resilient leaders also make fair judgments, share knowledge, retain integrity, develop others, and continue to grow throughout their lives. Resilient challenges are problems that experts are unable to solve. They necessitate in-house tests, findings, and changes. People must accept new values and attitudes, as well as absorb the change, in order to make the adaptive jump. Resilient leaders lead with empathy, learn from their mistakes, accept change, and create conditions that benefit the greatest number of people. Resilient leadership may help authority figures see the broad picture and delegate important work back to individuals and teams during times of crisis.

Nowadays, teams are formed swiftly and then disbanded just as quickly. They must promptly establish contact with the project leader, be given full authority to make choices, and complete the assignment. If agility is not fostered, inflexible leaders can severely slow down growth. The art of resilient leadership is establishing the ideal environment for self-organisation. An atmosphere in which agile teams cooperate, learn from one another, receive immediate feedback from users, and are committed to quality and continual improvement. In today's complicated VUCCAD (Volatile, uncertainty, complexity, conflicting, ambiguity, and dynamic) settings, striking a balance between chaos and rigorous structure is critical. It might be difficult to create and maintain the ideal environment. Culture, ownership, mentality, feedback, and long-term objectives are all important. The leader must be able to handle a variety of situations, particularly new, changing, and ambiguous ones.

"We cannot address the problems with the same mindset that created them," Einstein observed.

You are to blame for our current circumstances. Here's something to think about for a bit. Your systems have been tuned to provide the results you're seeing now. If your work efforts are constantly over budget or late, you've established a system that not only produces these results, but it is optimised to produce them. You must modify the system in order to change the outcomes. A resilient leader places a premium on value and respect. Each team member's input is valuable and appreciated. Adaptive leaders also take the time to listen. Resilient leaders often think about the best way to bring change to their team rather than imposing it all on them all at once. There are several parallels to the affiliate leadership style. It is possible to make too many changes in a short period of time.

Leaders frequently state that they favor transparency. What they truly mean is that they want to know what their teams are up to all of the time. Leaders who are honest about their own work—sharing information about what they're working on, bigger corporate goals, and the priorities that should direct their teams' work—are required for agile leadership. Resilient or Agile leaders make sure their employees are knowledgeable about the organisation's strategy and the context in which they operate, and then they step aside. Rather than checking in on their teammates, they check in. They also provide employees the freedom to work through concerns and solve problems.

How does today's resilient leader become ready for change?

For teams, resilient leadership necessitates new levels of empowerment, enablement, and development. Agile teams are learning new work practices at the same time as executives who are ensuring success in the new agile environment. Feedback is an important aspect of adaptive development. Great resilient leaders provide feedback while also empowering their teams to provide and accept input. They assist the team in maintaining contact with the organisation in order to obtain critical feedback from internal customers and the organisation as a whole. Resilient or agile leaders serve as mentors and coaches for the teams they manage. Customers must be involved in the process for agile work approaches to be successful. Great resilient leaders make it easier for customers to participate. Consumers' expectations are defined, opportunities and workplaces where customers may be present are provided, and customers are given the time they require. In fact, resilient leaders would not allow a team to start a project unless the customer was prepared to spend time with the team.

Measurement, monitoring, and management are all intertwined. Great resilient leaders encourage teams to measure their own results in addition to tracking their own measures. They track factors like meeting time, number of projects, customer happiness, team trust, and more, in addition to velocity, the gold standard of agile measurement. They know how the team is doing so they can provide feedback, eliminate roadblocks, and create possibilities for growth. Working on one project at a time, for example, is an important aspect of agile. Leaders must sometimes push back on the business to ensure that agile teams are not overburdened and can thrive by prioritising projects and outcomes. Performance is measured by resilient leaders. Because resiliency is a new method of working in most organisations, outstanding adaptive leaders must educate the rest of the organisation on work procedures, eliminate barriers, and establish team boundaries. Working as a team, for example, is an important aspect of resiliency.

Resilient leadership, poses a number of difficulties. Experimenting, learning new information, and making multiple modifications throughout your organisation are all part of this leadership paradigm. You will only be able to maintain the changes and prosper if you modify your mindset and adjust your policies. Changing people's attitudes, beliefs, and perceptions, on the other hand, is frequently more difficult than flossing a cat's teeth. Making adjustments necessitates a degree of disloyalty to your past. If you wish to adopt a new marketing plan, for example, you must first accept the truth that your current marketing techniques are ineffective.

Another issue with resilient leadership is that it creates an environment conducive to various types of opposition. This might be from your employees or other stakeholders in the organisation. Stakeholder Any individual, group, or entity with an interest in an organisation and the effects of its activities is referred to as a stakeholder in business. Marginalising, distracting, and assaulting are the most prevalent techniques used to stymie adaptive change. If you see any of these behaviors, it's likely that your employees are resisting the new policy you're attempting to impose.

Resilient leadership, poses a number of difficulties. Experimenting, learning new information, and making multiple modifications throughout your organisation are all part of this leadership paradigm. You will only be able to maintain the changes and prosper if you modify your mindset and adjust your policies. While maintaining a positive environment, resilient leadership may provide businesses with inventive and meaningful answers to challenging situations. Resilient leadership necessitates the participation of all members of the organisation. This implies resilient leaders must urge everyone engaged to change their mentality and display resilient leadership skills. Employees who prefer the status quo and have no desire to change the organisation may find this difficult.

The refusal of leaders to listen to other people's perspectives is perhaps the biggest obstacle posed by adaptive leadership. Adaptive leadership, as previously said, is more about cooperation than it is about power. Resilient leaders, in principle, should be open to listening to and modifying suggestions made by coworkers or clients. In actuality, only a small number of leaders are prepared to listen to others who disagree with them. What such leaders fail to realise is that listening does not always imply forsaking one's own objectives. It simply implies that you have a better understanding of your employees' requirements. As a result, you'll be able to work more efficiently to implement modifications. Resilient leaders foster a progressive and open-minded work environment. Errors are recognised as a necessary part of the process. Resilient leaders recognise and embrace adversity. They get their team members ready to solve problems. Resilient leaders recognise that finding a long-term solution may take a few tries.

Hesitancy change can only be successful if everyone in the organisation is involved in its execution. Some employees may be unwilling to execute a new approach because it requires them to master a new method or alters the nature of their work. It is possible that a new strategy will be unsuccessful if it is not applied across the whole organisation. Resilient leadership transfers authority and influence from a few top-level executives to all employees. Some top-level workers who are accustomed to wielding a great deal of decision-making authority may find it difficult to give control to the entire group. Resilient leaders value relationships as much as they value money.This knowledge aids them in ensuring that organisational members and other stakeholders are on board with any long-term changes. Although adaptive leadership demands a significant amount of work, it pays off handsomely. Resilient businesses, according to trustworthy statistics, reap enormous financial and operational benefits. Even during moments of turbulence, they are able to withstand storms and surge to the top.

Resilient leadership depends on the ability to bring together a broad collection of individuals to explore ideas and develop practical solutions. Long-term results are improved when there are more ideas. Team members can also benefit from one another's knowledge and experience by gaining some personal and professional growth. Resilient leaders adopt a democratic leadership style rather than a hierarchical one in this way. For the resilient leader, rules serve as a guideline rather than a strict manner of doing things. This leader is intent on attaining the best possible result in the most efficient manner possible. It may even become clear that the present regulations aren't working for the organisation and need to be changed.

A resilient leader places a premium on value and respect. Each team member's input is valuable and appreciated. Resilient leaders also take the time to listen. Resilient leaders often think about the best way to bring change to their team rather than imposing it all on them all at once. There are several parallels to the affiliate leadership style. It is possible to make too many changes in a short period of time. A resilient leader may terminate a failing initiative before it has a chance to prosper. This may not sit well with certain team members, resulting in a schism among the organisation's members. Discord is an impediment to successful transformation. Resilient leaders stay on top of the current trends so that they have a variety of methods to choose from when change is required. All strategies will fail to achieve the goals set by the leader. The leader, on the other hand, can swiftly adjust and identify the best approach for the situation.

The resilient leader recognises that change is a difficult process. As a result, he or she can anticipate and counteract any hesitant conduct on the part of colleagues. A recognition that large-scale change is a slow process that needs patience and a willingness to withstand the pressure that comes with it. Resilient leaders understand that change takes time and are willing to put in the time required to build a better organisation. Resilient leaders are proactive in their approach. They detect problems and spend whatever resources are required to remedy them ahead of time. Resilient leaders are at ease with the unknown. They understand that not having a quick solution to an issue is an important element of the positive transformation process. Resilient leaders enjoy experimenting with new ideas and solving problems. They are ready to evaluate their work and make adjustments as needed. They recognise that handling nebulous and difficult topics necessitates trial and error. Resilient leaders connect long-term corporate objectives to systematic transformation. Action is conducted with the goal of achieving a certain outcome in mind.

In terms of difficulty, resilient leadership can be distinguished. A technological problem may have a one-time solution, but an adaptive problem requires time and may necessitate organisational culture changes. The latter occurs when a organisation is in transition and needs to adjust its long-term business plans. Leadership that emphasises being ready and eager to work on changes has a lot of success.

"All fixed set patterns are incapable of resiliency or pliability. The truth is outside of all fixed patterns." -Bruce Lee

Several times in your career, you've been required to lead in an uncertain atmosphere. Situations in which everyone looked to you to make single-point-of-failure judgments based solely on your presumptions. During times of increased danger, the doctrine and chain of command were developed to support you via empirical direction. Many of the circumstances in which you were entrusted to serve proved to be much more challenging for your predecessors, who were well-known as excellent leaders. Unfortunately, the broad or core leadership style that your predecessors were known for failed miserably. Your success, was due to the growth of resilient leadership. When things go bad, an resilient leader helps stakeholders face the situation head-on rather than withholding. They encourage people to take part in problem-solving activities. People who are led by resilient leaders are encouraged to think for themselves and make their own judgments. They also exhibit confidence in people's ability to solve difficulties successfully. Providing the right amount of direction and structure helps stakeholders feel confident in their decisions as they negotiate adaptive issues.

A resilient leader recognises that ceding authority in this way allows out-group members to be more active, autonomous, and accountable for their own activities in the adaptive work of the organisation and can create more commitment on their part. Resilient leadership depends on the ability to bring together a broad collection of individuals to explore ideas and develop practical solutions. Long-term results are improved when there are more ideas. Team members can also benefit from one another's knowledge and experience by gaining some personal and professional growth. Resilient leaders adopt a democratic leadership style rather than a hierarchical one in this way.

What makes a great leader different from a poor leader?

The answer is straightforward: their capacity to quickly adapt to changing surroundings, rules, or ethical standards, as well as their ability to motivate their teams to embrace change by causing a major shift in their behaviors and attitudes. On the other hand, mediocre or ineffective leaders resist change and are unable to make the required modifications in a dynamic work environment, resulting in negativity, stagnation, and sluggishness. Let's look at a few situations of resilient leadership in action, where leaders used it to bring out the best in their staff, which ultimately helped the company as a whole.

Nisha was a capable, well-liked, and well-respected team leader. Her attitude towards work was professional but compassionate. She treated her workers as if they were family, yet she made no excuses when it came to getting the job done. Nisha resigned, and her departure was felt by everyone on the team. Soon later, a replacement was found. All of the team members were concerned about the new manager's ability to handle the squad; they believed the newcomer would never be able to fill Nisha's shoes. Because new manager realised he had huge shoes to fill, the new leader adopted an resilient approach. He had the option of leading from a position of power, but he decided not to. He solicited input and ideas from the team to ensure that they felt appreciated and respected, just as Nisha did.

Hence, If you adopt the usual route to tackling this problem, you may explore the following options: Perhaps you should provide extra bonuses and advantages to your staff. Perhaps you should give them a significant raise above their existing pay. Perhaps their managers need to work on improving their management abilities and motivating their employees.

This, however, is not how resilient leadership approaches a situation like this. The HR department elected to go deeper into the source of the problem, involving the entire senior management team in the investigation to see whether monetary rewards and other incentives were the true cause or whether something else was at play. The new manager proceeded to solicit new ideas from the staff on a regular basis. His team quickly came to trust and admire him for pushing intra-team collaboration to new levels. Over the course of his career, he effectively led the squad through ups and downs and experienced success.

If you want to be an resilient leader, you need to study, apply, and display four qualities: character, organisational justice, growth, and emotional intelligence. You have an excellent knowledge of your feelings and the feelings of people around you if you have high emotional intelligence.

You can respond to your team in a fair, calm, and compassionate manner if you have acquired emotional intelligence. Of course, there are many aspects to emotional intelligence, and being sympathetic, searching for emotional reactions, respecting people's feelings, and adjusting your actions to their feelings can bring you a long way in this area. Despite the fact that an resilient leader isn't scared to disobey the rules, he or she has a strong personality. This leader takes delight in being open, honest, and resourceful. The team respects the leader for owning up to his or her faults and making the appropriate decisions to repair them. The blame game isn't something an resilient leader has time for.

Task management is a strength of resilient leaders. After examining each individual's distinctive abilities and strengths, they allocate the appropriate individuals to the proper jobs. Resilient leaders empower their teams by providing them with tools and chances to improve their professional skills. Resilient leaders are skilled at detecting nonverbal clues and interpreting their colleagues' emotions. This ability enables them to comprehend others and steer their actions accordingly. Resilient leaders strive to get the greatest results in the simplest way feasible. They have the ability to bend or violate current structural rules to achieve the desired effects.

You can learn to be both an observer and a participant at the same time, fortunately. When you're at a meeting, practice by monitoring what's going on as it happens—even if you're a part of it. Examine the interactions to observe how people's attention to one another varies, whether it's supporting, thwarting, or listening. Keep an eye out for people's body language. When you make a point, fight the urge to sit on the edge of your seat, ready to defend what you've said. After you talk, a simple method like moving your chair a few inches away from the table may give you the real and metaphorical space you need to become an observer.

Leaders encourage others to reconsider their own priorities and examine any inconsistencies in their value system. Contradictions are usually resolved by placing them out of sight. When people in positions of leadership ask difficult questions and point out inconsistencies, they get neutralised. Effective leaders recognise and expect losses in the course of their work. Many individuals with strong ideas and moral convictions have a tendency to discount others who disagree with them rather than see the good in the opposing system. Effective leaders must be able to talk compassionately about the losses that individuals, organizations, and communities will suffer, as well as recognize the nobility in opposing systems.

As a leader, you must help people realize how what they gain is crucial to their basic beliefs and how the change will aid in the evolution of their traditions rather than depreciate them. Resilient leaders have a deep awareness of each employee's strengths and weaknesses, and they manage them appropriately. Resilient leaders have a high level of flexibility, i.e., the capacity to seamlessly go from traditional to adaptive leadership styles. Resilient leaders are driven to achieve excellent results and to infuse their enthusiasm and fire into their teams. Because they expect plans to alter, adaptive leaders always have contingency plans in place.

Another fundamental element of resilient leadership is to promote and nurture an honest culture. Resilient executives are well-versed in the finest policies that can be implemented to help the company. They can also efficiently execute such rules in a way that people accept them. Every employee feels appreciated and respected because their thoughts and ideas are heard and considered. As more new ideas are presented, this has a ripple effect across the business. This encourages more buy-in, which is necessary for the solution's effective implementation. Resilient leadership should provide their staff with the most up-to-date technologies to increase efficiency and production while reducing time and effort spent on various activities.

The problem works for the leader as much as the leader works for the problem.

Resilient leaders keep their heritage alive by refining or evolving it. If this growth hurts relationships , the ties must be renegotiated as part of the transformation process. Deeply held beliefs and identities may be impacted by these shifts. If these values and identities are thoroughly and compassionately addressed, change may strengthen rather than weaken the foundation on which the company or community was created.

Resilient leadership, like all leaders, is concerned with making big decisions. But what sets them apart as leaders is that they are open to input, prepared for inevitable change, adept at adapting to new situations, and flexible enough to reverse course when necessary.

CHAPTER THREE

Cultivating Greatness At Work By Building Organisational Culture Of Resilience

"Resiliency to changing circumstances is a must-have attribute for today's businesses, especially in this unpredictable environment."

We are in a dynamic and quick-paced era. In order to sustain operations and a competitive edge, organisations have transformed quickly. Due to these disruptions, both customers and employees have undergone changes that are reflected in their tastes and social behaviours. Additionally, the recent advent of technology and technologies to streamline procedures, particularly during the pandemic, has had a significant influence on the workforce and changed how organisations operate.

"Learn to adjust yourself to the conditions you have to endure, but make a point of trying to alter or correct conditions so that they are most favorable to you."
-William Frederick Book

The majority of organisational challenges you confront are caused by gaps between how organisations actually operate and how you believe they work. As a result of feedback, these things get more aligned. It is the leader's responsibility to foster a culture that values and changes in response to input. Failure must be considered a chance to learn. To compete, people must be encouraged to try and retest their ideas, as well as given room to iterate. This is adaptation, and resilient organisations are the result of resilient leadership.

Change is unavoidable.

Because the world is changing at a breakneck pace, leaders come in a variety of sizes and forms. If you've been keeping up with the newest leadership trends, you've definitely already heard about several techniques and ideals that have proven successful for many current and prospective business leaders. To be honest, there is no right or wrong way to lead, as long as you have the best interests of your team and your organisation at heart. But what if your squad isn't going to stay the same for long? It will shift. And it's not only your team that will alter; it's your workplace culture, your market, everything. This is when you put one of your essential leadership characteristics, namely resiliency, to the test.

In this chapter, I'll offer some statistics on why and how resiliency is a critical component of leadership, regardless of the team or organisation with which you're working. In addition, you'll discover some of my finest ideas and methods for being a resilient leader in a fast-paced sector. Most significantly, flexibility is changing to suit new conditions and obstacles, which will ensure your organisation's or organisation's success. Why is it vital for a leader to be resilient? Everything grows and evolves into something better, including the workplace dynamic, corporate strategy, and technological advancements. Adapting and responding is the only way to survive as a leader and face the complexity of change, whether you like it or not.

An organisation that can function effectively in unforeseen conditions can adopt whole new approaches. Such businesses have the technology, manpower, and tools to outperform the competition at any moment. Resilient organisations are better suited to lead and set the pace for a whole industry. A resilient organisation is always better suited to meet difficulties and deal with adversity. People in such settings are more resilient and have a renewed willingness to face challenges. They are more capable of drifting through problems quickly as a consequence of their grit.

"Resiliency is built on innovation, and encouraging individuals to think outside the box is critical to achieving it."

Resiliency is essential to generating progress and helps the organisation and its members stay effective and productive through times of change and uncertainty. Leaders must not only be flexible themselves, but they must also be able to detect adaptation in their employees. This ability aids leaders in selecting individuals who are best suited to change-related work and who can motivate and serve as role models for others during the transition period that comes with any new project.

Resiliency is therefore critical to the effectiveness and success of leaders. This is most likely not breaking news to you. Despite the fact that the need for resiliency in leaders is now widely accepted, little is understood about what resiliency actually entails. Little research has been done on the specific behaviors that define resiliency up to now. If leaders can obtain a better understanding of these behaviors, they will be able to not only recognise them but also take the first steps toward creating flexibility in themselves and others. Many executives fail due to their inability or unwillingness to change. This could be due to their incapacity or unwillingness to adapt their management style, as well as their personal fear of change.

"The only way to behave wisely is to reflect on both accomplishments and mistakes and share lessons learned with all employees."

Given the chaotic and uncertain global climate that organisations confront on both a macro and local level, planning for the future has never been more challenging. When the dust settles from the COVID-19 problem, you might be confronted with a new environment that may differ radically from what you are used to in terms of consumer behavior, business models, and the responsibilities of the public and private sectors. The longer and more severe the crisis, the more likely it is that dramatic changes will characterise the new world of tomorrow. I have highlighted the variety of probable situations businesses may encounter, as well as guidelines and best practices for making strategic decisions in tomorrow's new environment, based on insights from client interactions and internal specialists.

Why do some people succeed while others don't?

Organisations cannot go back to the way things were before because the genie is out of the bottle. Leaders and organisations will continue to experience the effects of COVID for years to come. You are not alone if you are now experiencing the pressure and strain of leadership. A different and more complicated environment is posing challenges to many leaders.

Resilient leadership is the key to succeeding in this new environment for leaders. However, what exactly is resilient leadership, and why is it so crucial? How can you develop your leadership resilience so that you can prosper in difficult, disruptive, and turbulent circumstances? Resilient leaders may maintain their vigour in stressful situations. so that they are able to adjust to disruptive developments. They recover quickly after failures. They also overcome significant obstacles without acting dysfunctionally or hurting other people.

Resiliency necessitates effective change interpretation, and the first step is admitting that change has occurred. The important parts of the transition that successful adapters address are how a new vision will produce new markets, competitors, and organisational positions. It's also crucial to figure out how the change will affect the organisation's operations. Another facet of cognitive flexibility is the ability to generate alternative strategies. Resilient leaders may let go of old roles and concepts, recognise and embrace new roles, and devise new tactics and action plans to meet the consequences of the transition and the current situation.

Divergent thinking is another aspect of cognitive flexibility, such as considering a completely new approach that turns a change into an advantage, or recognising and putting to use the skills of new team members. Finally, cognitive adapters excel at transcending organisational boundaries; they analyse how the change will affect others and disseminate this knowledge to various organisational units and senior management.

Resiliency is a must-have organisational attribute for business executives.

Leaders that are resilient are keenly aware of external disruptions and psychologically ready to come out on top. Colonel Sanders would not have created KFC, Thomas Edison would not have created the electric lightbulb, and Albert Einstein would not have developed the theory of relativity if they had given up. As a result, all of these legendary figures managed outside distractions while continuing in their endeavours throughout their beliefs. Threats were turned into opportunities, and they ultimately made everything possible. Strong leaders don't point the finger at others. They assume accountability for their deeds and inspire hope in others.

It is the outcome of a comprehensive viewpoint. You may use it to grow comfortable being uncomfortable and support it with a network of positive interpersonal and professional connections. Resilience draws on your capacity for adaptation while also relying on your understanding of who you are as a person—your beliefs, self-assurance, and optimism. Make it a crucial component of your success as a leader on all fronts, from your pursuit of personal objectives and wellbeing to your capacity to guide people during periods of change, stress, and uncertainty.

If you could control this inner critic, how much more effective and optimistic would you be?

Self-help gurus and scientists frequently contend that worrying excessively and robbing ourselves of the moment may be sources of stress and sorrow. It has been demonstrated that mindfulness practises like meditation improve our moods and general wellness. You are probably familiar with the inner voice that never stops talking. It is constantly compelled to criticise, compare, and appraise everything as either excellent or terrible. It continually disrupts your ability to focus, think clearly, and make decisions. This voice frequently gets in the way of your potential to be a resilient leader.

You can control your inner critic by engaging in mindfulness and meditation activities. The two straightforward methods that follow might be useful if you are new to these procedures. The next time you have an uncomfortable idea, such as one that makes you feel horrible, guilty, inferior, anxious, or any other negative emotion, stop and let the thought or sensation simply be without attempting to oppose it or criticise it. If your experience is anything like mine, the thought or emotion will just go. Stay with it if you don't see this outcome right away. It works.

How to make a resilient organisation?

As the global economy returns to normal, it's an exciting moment to be a white-shoe advisor, working with struggling businesses that need all the support they can get with growth, expenses, strategy, and execution. If there was ever any doubt about the importance of a leader's capacity to negotiate change, uncertainty, and disruption, the worldwide pandemic of 2020 proved it beyond a shadow of a doubt. While you all wish to avoid future pandemics, one thing is certain: you will not be able to escape increased complexity. Rather than avoiding these sentiments, you must learn to accept and embrace them as an inevitable component of the learning process. According to Microsoft CEO Satya Nadella, executives must move from a "know it all" to a "learn it all" approach. This adjustment in perspective might assist in alleviating the discomfort by relieving the strain on you to know everything.

The ability of managers to deal with this type of transition—losing familiar team members and dealing with new and unknown colleagues—has a significant impact on organisational efficiency and production. Change – and how they and their colleagues react to it – has become critical to their effectiveness and the success of their businesses, as leaders are well aware. In a poll conducted by Ernst & Young and Cap Gemini Ernst & Young, 86 CEOs identified the top three dangers that they and their businesses would face in the future years. Executives (19%) mentioned regulatory changes (38%), competitive dynamics (29%), and market uncertainty. All of these issues are linked to the transition.

New initiatives can be derailed or stifled before they get a chance, or just die on the vine, if leaders don't consider their own resiliency and that of their subordinates. When an organisation's top leadership announces a new vision, for example, managers and their teams are expected to embrace it and propel it toward implementation as rapidly as feasible. to comprehend and embrace the new vision, as well as to motivate subordinates to follow suit.

It is critical for everyone to understand their role in delivering value to make an organisation more resilient. Every member of the team is responsible for ensuring the organisation's success. Everyone must take the initiative and behave as a leader. It all begins with the board of directors agreeing that this is the sort of culture they want to see developed. Following agreement, specific procedures must be performed to begin the implementation process. Leaders and managers must collaborate. Leaders and managers must work hard to build a culture of choice, which may be aided by having a description of the current culture in place. A description that may be used for this purpose is as follows:

- A clear and unmistakable mission, presented as a simple "big idea" to which all employees can relate and are eager to communicate with employees.
- An atmosphere of shared responsibility for the organisation's future success, in which all employees are encouraged to think independently, be sensitive to one another, be kind and supportive of one another, and behave with humanity.
- Working in teams that are places of mutual support, where everything is contested without fear of humiliation, where critique of individual and team work is encouraged, addressed, and lessons are learned and applied, are all examples of psychologically responsible behavior.
- Employees who exude confidence in their clients and customers, who "go the extra mile" by sharing unsolicited ideas, thoughts, and stimuli, and whose interest in their customers extends beyond respect and service, delivering attentiveness and personal

involvement.

- Leaders and supervisors that push their employees, create opportunities for personal growth via new experiences, and treat everyone fairly and with empathy

Many corporate executives continue to assume that conventional market dominance indicators give them an unbeatable competitive edge. However, as the rate of disruption increases, it becomes clear that the largest and "strongest" business operators are not always the ones that will survive. As the epidemic progressed, this had become increasingly obvious, with many organisations, large and small, battling to withstand the COVID-19 disruption and its long-term consequences.

In ways never seen before, the COVID-19 pandemic had increased the pace of disruption and exposed the degree of globalisation and the interconnectedness of technology, business, and society. This transition had also exposed the volatility of individuals formerly regarded as industry leaders.

Resiliency is essential for an organisation's ability to respond successfully to changing business conditions. Almost every organisation plans how to function when business conditions are predictable, but the key to long-term survival is being able to adapt successfully to the unexpected.

No organisation is immune to disruption.

Many businesses have been pushed to their limits, and in some cases, to the brink of bankruptcy, in the previous year. Today, no sector or organisation is immune to disruption, but many are unprepared to adapt rapidly enough to keep up with the pace of change. Their systems have disintegrated due to intense strain on operations, supply chains, and demand, and any notion of collaboration among their ranks has been tossed to the wind. Working in crisis mode is, of course, neither sustainable nor desirable. Many organisation executives are now wondering how they can maintain momentum post-crisis and ensure their organisations‘ future resiliency.

"Change is good. It's also often hard. But to succeed in business, you must run toward it."

What makes today's corporate environment unique is how ubiquitous dynamism is. The rate of change is now affecting everyone, not just the so-called disrupted industries or particular aspects of your organisation; it's occurring in every industry and at every level of business. Because technology is so ingrained in every aspect of our operations, it is at the center of much of the changing environment. Technology changes the way you communicate, market, drive your business processes, shape product development and manufacturing, and determines how you connect with your customers for many organisations. However, it isn't having the greatest technology that gives you a competitive edge; it's enterprises that adapt technology to fit their strategic goals.

In 2022, global businesses plan to become more resilient in response to rising digital experience expectations. While 90% of CEOs believe their organisation must be able to adapt quickly and at scale in order to provide value to their customers, consumers continue to perceive brands as falling short. According to the report, 91% of corporate leaders have made efforts to enhance customer experiences in the last year, with 84% undertaking more experimentation than ever during the epidemic, testing and iterating to discover what worked and what didn't. While 9 out of 10 respondents believe their organisation must be able to adapt quickly and on a large scale in order to provide value to customers, only half (46%) believe they are already resilient.

Furthermore, 78% of consumers believe businesses could do a better job of changing to match current demands. 70% of corporate executives agree that they cannot optimize as soon as they would want, and roughly the same number 72% express difficulty scaling efforts to suit global demands, highlighting the disparity between brands' objectives and purpose in relation to the adaptive digital experience they presently offer.

"You can't build an adaptable organisation without adaptable people--and individuals change only when they have to, or when they want to." -Gary Hamel

Many interrelated aspects make up complex tasks, some of which are unknown and alter in unanticipated ways over time. Furthermore, an action or change in one dimension might have unintended and exaggerated consequences. While there are many points of view on these issues, no obvious answers exist. As a result, complex problem-solving solutions are usually discovered by trial and error and need the desire, humility, and capacity to act, learn, and adapt. Many high achievers have an action bias and grow dissatisfied fast when confronted with problems for which there is no obvious answer or clear line of action. Leaders must not give in to the need for a rapid answer.

To weather the inevitably coming storms, business needs strong leaders. They also need a lot of human ingenuity and invention. Innovative measures led by strong leaders will be necessary to sustainably revive the economy. So go ahead and learn to be comfortable with discomfort.

Long-term success requires resiliency. It is critical to survive in turbulent times , when the world was in the grip of a worldwide epidemic. Because few of them failed to adapt to the ever-changing business landscape, giants such as Myspace, Kodak, and RadioShack are now just memories. According to McKinsey, 84% of business owners regard innovation as being critical to their development strategy, and 80% fear failure in the near future if they are unable to adapt to changing economic conditions. Walt Disney CEO Bob Iger once said that, "Innovate or perish." With their inventive ideas and capacity to resilient to quick changes, leaders establish trends and flourish in marketplaces. Clients trust them more than those that simply follow trends and produce imitations of innovative products or services.

"Resiliency is a feature that can lead to the development of other desirable attributes in people and organisations."

The COVID-19 epidemic hastened the pace of change, highlighting the degree of globalisation and the interconnectedness of technology, society, and the environment in new ways. This paradigm change has also exposed the frailty of individuals formerly regarded as industry leaders. However, not all businesses have faltered throughout the epidemic. Some businesses, such as so-called "work from home" businesses and e-commerce giants, were in the right place at the right time. Others have managed to stay afloat thanks to a strong emphasis on resilience, financial stability, and contingency preparation. Even fewer have strategically leveraged the crisis to develop or grow their businesses. These businesses have shown an exceptional capacity to adapt swiftly to changing conditions. Such businesses are ideally positioned to compete in the present, future, and beyond.

How can people transition from crisis mode to proactive thinking?

The epidemic has brought attention to the need for businesses to be adaptive, but business executives have long recognised this requirement. They had to deal with various problems even before the chaos of 2020. Most corporate executives believe they have been in a perpetual state of "transformation" for the past two decades, and many are weary of hearing the phrase. The secret is to maintain a constant state of flexibility. Every business leader understands that in order to thrive in the long run, their organisation must adapt. The true challenge isn't effectively converting your organisation on a one-time basis; it's writing the capacity to adapt and transform into the DNA of the organisation. It's about creating a mechanism or reaction to cope with any crisis that arises, whether it's a financial, technical, environmental, or health-related one.

Many of the leaders you engage with express feelings of isolation as a result of the constant change and unpredictability in their situations. Part of their sense of isolation stems from an underlying notion that they must solve all of their problems on their own. Your natural instinct is to increase your attention and individual efforts as the complexity and volume of your tasks grow. This can be a successful method when dealing with relatively short-term difficulties with well-known answers. It may be disastrous, however, when faced with difficulties when the whole scale of issues and interdependencies, let alone solutions, is unknown. Instead, now is the time to create the habit of purposefully reaching out to your network and beyond for advice and information. The difficulty is that, despite the effort put out by business executives, most attempts to make organisations adaptive fail. My personal experience working in management and as a strategy consultant supports this. When you ask senior executives what went wrong, you'll hear the same concerns again and over: Some employees inside the organisation neglected to accept responsibility for the transition process. People began blaming one another. Nothing was done about it when things went wrong. The metamorphosis slowed down over time.

For many resilient organisations, profit plans have been replaced by promises of organisation continuity. Many businesses put long-term aspirations on hold to meet the needs of a workforce concerned about their future, stakeholders facing unpredictable demands, and operational obstacles. The challenge of labor planning is mitigated to some extent in industries where remote employment is available. However, it will necessitate more unlearning and upskilling. While some businesses balked at the new expectations owing to a lack of digital preparedness, purpose-driven businesses maintained spirits high and order volumes high by delivering online.

The issue is that tighter restrictions may suffocate an organisation. In truth, management should relinquish control and allow the business the flexibility it requires to function efficiently. The concept is that management should focus on stating their goals and letting the organisation figure out how to get there. It might be difficult to let go of your grasp while not allowing the organisation to fall apart. It must be founded on a defined set of concepts that are supported by science.

As the speed of change in businesses accelerates, most managers and administrators will need to be more flexible and resilient in their leadership. Increased globalisation and international commerce; rapid technological change; changing cultural values; a more diverse workforce; more outsourcing; new forms of social networking; increased use of virtual interaction; more visibility of leadership actions; and concern for outcomes other than profits are examples of changes that increase the need for flexibility, adaptation, and innovation by leaders. Although there is currently a lack of studies specifically focused on flexible and resilient leadership, interest in the topic is growing as its value becomes more apparent.

Furthermore, because subordinates differ in terms of experience, talents, beliefs, and requirements, a leader's conduct with various individuals should vary. For subordinates with good talents and a strong dedication to work objectives, for example, increased delegation is suitable. When a subordinate's talents and motivations vary over time, flexibility is also essential. Using the same scenario, greater delegation will be acceptable as a subordinate acquires experience and confidence.

Different sorts of management jobs, as well as positions in another organisation with a diverse objective or culture, require different patterns of conduct for effective leadership. Making these job transfers successfully is another sign of flexible and resilient leadership. Finding inventive methods to cope with new issues and possibilities is frequently part of being flexible and resilient, yet the sorts of decisions and actions required for effective leadership may not be compatible with standard organisational position expectations. Role expectations can sometimes be founded on outdated ideas or inappropriate norms and values (e.g., gender role stereotypes, centralised authority, intolerance for any failures, or promotion based on seniority rather than performance). It may be necessary for a leader to persuade individuals to shift their assumptions and views about what is proper and successful in order to extend their options, especially when the benefits of creative techniques are not immediately apparent.

These real-world circumstances have a role in organisational transformation, allowing flexible businesses to make progress while others struggle to establish ground rules and goals. You can sense the difference when you come into a high-performing organisation. People are energised rather than going through the motions. Rather than being puzzled or resigned, they are confident in their organisation's direction and the changes that are taking place. They understand what they are meant to be doing and how it connects to their neighbors' activities. Checking performance measurements like sustained profitability and market share growth at organisations, as well as social impact in the charity arena, can swiftly validate your informal findings.

But how do businesses become high-performance businesses? We all know that organisational and people skills drive financial and operational success and enable organisations to execute their plans, yet the majority of businesses have no idea how to quantify them. Tolstoy was correct: each sad family is miserable in its own unique manner, while all happy families—or high-performing organisations—are the same. All businesses may place themselves in a better position to succeed by knowing the common strands of organisational DNA.

Organisational design may assist businesses in improving

execution and achieving strategic objectives. However, the interaction of its essential elements—structure, personal talents, responsibilities, and collaboration—must be properly organised and intimately integrated with a organisation's strategy and sources of competitive advantage for this to happen.

The management of bad performers is the polar opposite of talent management. The way a organisation manages the development or departure of low-performing individuals sends a strong message to the rest of the organisation about what will be tolerated and praised.

Talent management is a far larger function than most businesses believe. It isn't just for those who are on the fast track. It also addresses the people and jobs that are crucial to a organisation's success. Relationship managers in financial brokerages and diagnostic testers in medical laboratories, for example, must be considered as valuable employees, even if they will never be in positions of leadership. These important jobs and people are identified by high-performance businesses, which then center retention tactics and contingency plans around them. This list of people and jobs should be fluid, altering in response to the organisation's strategic goals.

HR is a strategic partner and a business enabler. People strategy is as important as business strategy in leading organisations.People strategy is as important as business strategy in leading organisations. Through people initiatives, the HR department has successfully transformed business strategy into people objectives and supported business priorities. Strategic, functional, and transactional activities are clearly separated within the function. It effectively completes functional and transactional tasks while also influencing strategic issues. Many organisations may need to alter their HR skills to be able to supply line managers with data and advice in order to execute these various jobs and become strategic partners.

The capacity to evolve in two key ways creates a persistent competitive advantage in today's fast-paced environment. To begin, businesses must take a methodical approach to driving changes in focus, strategy, direction, structure, and culture. Second, they must have the ability to quickly respond to changing market conditions.

The structure is progressive. High-performance businesses are resilient, sensing market shifts and making strategic adjustments on the fly. The broad strokes of traditional strategy are supplemented rather than replaced by this approach. They provide their organisations' peripheries—far from the traditional strategy function—the authority to act in response to market changes.

Conventional organisations, the person in charge of making operational choices, particularly major ones, is the person at the top. The leader of flexible organisations works on creating the suitable atmosphere. In the case of the airport, the board's ability to focus on finding the best pilots and co-pilots while resisting the urge to co-design solutions was absolutely extraordinary. They trusted their staff, gradually let go of the reins in a measured manner, and were rewarded with powerful, inventive ideas that came from within the organisation.

Resilientbusinesses value themselves and the environment in which they operate. They don't strive to separate themselves from this environment; instead, they thrive in it. Survivors are highly adaptive groups. They were the ones that embraced change before it wrecked them, riding the wave while others battled against it. Resilientorganisations are those that not only survive a change in the hope of flowing back into serenity in the current economic conditions, which are crippled by numerous lockdowns and heaving under changing restrictions every few weeks. Organisational flexibility, on the other hand, allows them to accept more of these changes and make them work by altering their working model to meet the new requirements.

The encouraging reality is that people who have been dealing with fear and uncertainty for more than a year demonstrate an unbreakable spirit. Adaptive organisations' teams didn't rely on adrenaline; instead, they pushed themselves forward, appreciative of the positions they had and what they could do online if they couldn't meet their coworkers in person. To make teleworking feasible, business agility was followed to the letter and in spirit; a variety of virtual collaboration technologies were extensively utilised; and figures were tracked with the same earnestness as before the epidemic. Several of the flexible working concepts and policy modifications implemented during the pivotal period of uncertainty and emergency firefighting are still in place. Why? simply because they provide outcomes and keep flexible businesses on track with progress.

What are the building blocks of resilient organisations?

- Clients and stakeholders are frequently concerned that sensitive information may fall into the wrong hands when teams access databases remotely. For major enterprises or even small businesses to contemplate workforce flexibility, additional levels of security in the form of masking, network support, and encryption are essential.
- Crash courses and hands-on learning, which are typically done alone, provide the vital aspect of adaptation to this massive shift in working and engagement styles. The youthful workforce in India is fearless of change. According to a study, 53% of workers would consider changing occupations if it meant more flexibility on the job.
- Trust is more fundamental than any other aspect of an organisation's code of ethics. Employees that are trustworthy appreciate the challenge and honor of being a valued part of an organisation's day-to-day struggles and accomplishments. They repay the confidence placed in them by demonstrating their commitment to the organisation when it is most in need.
- When everything is up in the air, individuals are stronger when they stick together and help one another in modest steps toward a common goal. These modifications should be led by designated changemakers. Honest debates and even spontaneous exchanges of ideas can aid in the advancement of change.
- Experiment, test, and record change: It's no secret that in times of significant change, flexible businesses rely on essential individuals they can trust. It takes more than a strong willingness to ride through change to turn it into a consistent, practical model with a roadmap and

quantifiable goals.

- Using everyone's abilities rather than simply those of top-level leaders is what an ideal talent mix includes.
- A clear charter ensures that the organisation or team adheres to well-defined goals, responsibilities, and ground rules, while trust fosters strong links between employees, employers, and clients.
- There are various paradigms and definitions of leadership agility. The paradigm of one distinctive leadership style is slipping away in current times, and each scenario will require a different sort of leader. The team's agility is becoming increasingly important.

As a result, leadership agility is built on an adaptive team that can pivot in a new direction as the situation requires. Nowadays, teams are formed swiftly and then disbanded just as quickly. They must promptly establish contact with the project leader, be given full authority to make choices, and complete the assignment. If agility is not fostered, inflexible leaders can severely slow down growth.

"We cannot address the problems with the same mindset that created them," -Einstein observed.

You are to blame for your current circumstances. Here's something to think about for a bit. Your systems have been tuned to provide the results you're seeing now. If your work efforts are constantly over budget or late, you've established a system that not only produces these results, but it is optimised to produce them. You must modify the system in order to change the outcomes. The art of adaptive leadership is establishing the ideal environment for self-organisation. An atmosphere in which adaptive teams cooperate, learn from one another, receive immediate feedback from users, and are committed to quality and continual improvement. He or she neither micromanages nor creates unlimited freedom for the individuals.

Adaptive challenges require new learning and can only be addressed by changing people's assumptions, beliefs, habits, and allegiances. Technical problems can be very complex and important, but the solutions are known and can be solved by deploying already available expertise, processes, and operating procedures, such as a medical problem solved by surgery. Expertise and prior knowledge can aid in the resolution of adaptive challenges, but the most important task is to mobilise and guide individuals through a time of discovery that leads to a revitalised ability to thrive. Culture shifts after mergers or societal revolutions such as civil rights are examples.

Resiliency to shifting situations is a must-have attribute for organisations in today's unpredictable environment. Businesses may learn from nature's transformation playbook to become more flexible in an increasingly complex and unpredictable world. It is becoming increasingly obvious that all species' ability to recognise change and promptly adapt to it is more crucial than ever. Businesses may learn how to survive and prosper in the face of increasing change and unpredictability by looking to nature for inspiration. The underlying purpose of the individuals in these systems—creatures and enterprises alike—is to survive. This is one of the most striking parallels between nature and business.

Business leaders must prioritise flexibility as a must-have organisational attribute if they want to position themselves for long-term success in this changing climate. Traditional metrics of business health are no longer sufficient. To become resilient now and survive tomorrow, they must shift their mindset and transform swiftly and at scale, but how?

Many corporate executives continue to assume that conventional market dominance indicators give an unbeatable competitive edge. However, data shows that when disruption intensifies, the largest and "strongest" business organisations are not always the most likely to survive. As the epidemic progressed, things became increasingly obvious, and many businesses, large and small, tried to cope with the COVID-19 disruption and its consequences.

Survival is more important than transformation.

For every organisation, transformation simply means continuous progress. You, like sharks, must keep swimming in order to survive. The world changes all the time; customers' issued statements shift, risk profiles shift, and business models shift. As a result, you must change to stay up with the times. That has been our strategy since the beginning. Transformation has not been simple and will continue to be difficult. In today's ever-changing business market, you must remain relevant and take aggressive initiatives to ensure that you stay ahead of the curve.

However, the transformation does not produce instant, demonstrable results, especially in the face of increased organisation expenses and the introduction of several identical items, disturbing market equilibriums. Workforce transformation is required for organisation change to be successful. Existing employees needed to be retrained, and new employees with strong technical and engineering backgrounds needed to be recruited to help with the change. Businesses that do not change and adapt may not be able to survive in the long run. Business owners are forced to explore how to pivot their business models for the future.

"Finding the appropriate combination of challenge and support is the art of leader development."

In today's extremely dynamic climate, thriving, and possibly even surviving, demands ongoing, future-focused work that allows you to prepare and react to the change and uncertainty that lie ahead. Businesses that are proactive and strategic in managing their adaptive efforts will be the most successful. This entails adapting your business to changes in your ecosystem as well as adopting opportunities within the ecosystem to assist your organisation in changing for the better. The speed of change in today's business climate is faster than it has ever been, as practically every business book now published will tell you. However, this has been the case for decades. The present environment has been more dynamic than ever before for a long time.The most difficult problem is changing people's attitudes. The majority of people dislike change. Your most difficult task was persuading people who did not realise they needed to adapt even more quickly. You collected everyone who was excited about your transition and turned them into internal champions to help rouse the troops. Another problem is determining the proper technology and making the choice to adopt it. The most recent technology may not be the best option because it is not always reliable and suitable for use in our clients' environments. As a result, evaluating the most appropriate security solutions for your clients must be done methodically, taking into account their risk assessment, budget, operational requirements and demands, as well as technology.

Businesses can no longer wait to investigate a market trend

or new opportunity until the market – or a competitor – has proved that it is a safe path to take. By the time you notice that a business move is‘ safe ’for the majority, it has already progressed to the point where your organisation is struggling to stay afloat. Following a corporate trend or hopping on a technical bandwagon, on the other hand, is rarely an appropriate approach. Worse, you risk causing unforeseen repercussions that will take years to correct. Importantly, most organisations adopt a risk-based approach to change, in which they only accept the presence of an issue or danger when it becomes a big problem or threat, showing itself as a bad economic performance outcome.

Reacting to change in this manner puts you at risk of falling behind in a race that penalises those who can't keep up. They create outside-in and inside-out technology adaptations. It's all too tempting to get caught up in accepting technical change for the sake of embracing technological change—to adapt your organisation to the outside technological environment. However, the most successful organisations adapt to emerging technology to meet their internal demands, such as strategic goals and operating environments. This results in two-way adaptation, with business direction being used to analyse the possible implications of changing business landscapes and adjustments in that landscape being used to decide the path of future organisation directions.

Loss, not change, is what people and human systems fight against. Adaptive problems are difficult to overcome since change always entails a sense of loss. Any change endeavor needs leadership with the capacity to diagnose what losses will be suffered. Adaptive change that works does not discard the past, but rather builds on it. Adaptive challenges aren't only about change; they're also about keeping things going. As a result, leaders must also determine the critical aspects that must be maintained. Diversity enhances the ability to adapt and occurs as a result of exploration.

Many organisations managed to modify their operations models throughout the pandemic, according to McKinsey & Co., with the development of remote work. Businesses that had a successful transformation were more likely to perform in the top quartile of their peers. Businesses that did not invest in change, on the other hand, fared the poorest. This just goes to demonstrate that adaptability is the key to future success. It's vital to remember that resilient capability is a continuum. Some leaders (and organizations) are considered inherently nimble, while others must work hard to improve their adaptability. However, in the long term, the efforts to overcome any barriers will be worthwhile. All HR executives need to do now is get the rest of the firm on the same page.

First, HR executives must explain why agility and resiliency are so important for success, and leaders must recognize the need of resilient capability leadership. Then, and only then, should executives be encouraged to think about the company's operational model. Is it assisting and connecting teams rather than hindering them? Is it going to pave the road for a prosperous future? Finally, HR professionals should collaborate with corporate leaders to guarantee that the transition takes fewer than 18 months to accomplish. This, according to McKinsey & Co., will maintain momentum and prevent the organization from becoming exhausted.One such disruption is the proliferation of consumer options and the use of digital technology to differentiate them. It brings with it new opportunities as well as new problems. It's not enough to use digital technology on the periphery.

"The improvisational ability to lead resiliently relies on responding to the present situation rather than importing the past into the present and laying it on the current situation like an imperfect template. Knowing how the environment is pulling your strings and playing you is critical to making responsive rather than reactive moves."— Ronald Heifetz

Many of the modifications you made necessitated finding the correct balance of elements, maintaining tensions, and avoiding either or thinking. What do resilient leaders do in this situation? They made continuous improvement approaches work by giving them a purpose, fostering the necessary dispositions in adults, and providing the time, political space, relational environment, and learning culture. Developing a shared goal like this necessitates a high level of leadership ability. Finding something that fits perceived needs, is compatible with the expectations of the external world, and advances the improvement agenda ahead is the skill of determining the focus of an endeavor. Sometimes the purpose emerges from the needs of team and it's leader; in this case, the leader's responsibility is to listen and distill some shared aims, much like a community organizer might. The motivation might come from anywhere.

Consider yourself the HR Director of an organisation with a significant turnover rate. Employees that are highly trained and competent are leaving the company for rivals, which has a negative impact on the bottom line. What strategy would you use to tackle this problem? If you approach this scenario as a technological problem, you might be inclined to use technical solutions to fix it. Perhaps you require a new incentive scheme to keep your top employees? Perhaps they require more frequent rewards? Perhaps their bosses aren't doing a good job of encouraging and engaging them, and they need to improve. You could attempt these remedies and discover that they either don't work or just work for a short period of time.

People in organisations and politicians face similar challenges and pressures. However, it is anticipated that in public organisations such as legislatures, individuals will raise genuine concerns. In most other companies, this level of transparency is frowned upon. Resilient leaders must understand the importance of politics and think in terms of politics. The idea is to recognise that your employees are working hard to satisfy the expectations of their numerous stakeholders and constituencies. Only until you grasp the nature of these expectations, as well as each stakeholder's potential to affect the situation, unique set of desires and requirements, and intended results, can you mobilise effectively.

Organisations, like individuals, frequently have a misalignment between their espoused values and how they actually behave. According to research, the human brain reacts more to what a person does than to what they say they want to do. As a result, these behavioral patterns have become de facto organisational standards. When faced with competing commitments, those in positions of power must make judgments that result in losses for some and gains for others. Organisational leaders, on the other hand, frequently dodge these difficult decisions or try to find a solution that benefits no one.

Utilise the expertise and experience of the people who are on the frontlines of delivering business value—servicing your customers, developing what you manufacture, or sustaining your day-to-day organisation operations—while you investigate technology advances. Then enlist the help of those who are most knowledgeable about the technology to see what's achievable. Rather than requiring businesses to adapt to new technologies, technology facilitates commercial value. Business transition has long been associated with the organisation's strategy alterations. Business transformation is no longer an option in today's cause-and-effect society. Whether you like it or not, your organisation reacts to this changing dynamic. Your task is to steer that transformation in the right direction. Whether you like it or not, your organisation reacts to this changing dynamic. Your task is to take charge of that transformation and provide an opportunity to adjust to bad circumstances before they have a detrimental influence on you and your bottom line.

The corporate climate is extremely dynamic and demanding on a worldwide scale. There is fierce rivalry. To maintain your advantage, you must move a bit quicker than the opposition. There is uncertainty everywhere, making it difficult to anticipate what will happen next. Additionally, there is no guarantee that the choices you make will result in positive consequences. CEOs and executives have a difficult time outperforming their competitors. They find it more difficult to anticipate technological advancements. Building resilient organisations on a global scale is essential if we want to compete. Building resilient teams and leaders who can create resilient businesses that can outperform the competition and guarantee sustainability is demanded.

Ford was on the verge of bankruptcy when Alan Mulally took over and guided it to success, credibility, and stability. It is a remarkable business turnaround tale that combines financial austerity with a cultural shift in the car sector. It is the perfect case study for management grads everywhere. Lou Gerstner is a tenacious leader who successfully revived IBM via disciplined execution and a concentrated effort. By opposing leaders who are ruled by men, Carly Fiorina broke the glass ceiling. She was the first woman to run Hewlett-Packard, a Fortune 20 corporation (HP). Similar to this, one of the biggest US book shops, Borders, shut down in 2011. Why did these businesses, which at first had strong brands, ultimately fail? They failed to adjust to change, which is why.

In both calm and stormy times, the leaders must not only welcome change but also take the initiative to drive it. They are better able to avoid disruptive situations inside the workplace by being psychologically flexible. Therefore, in order to accomplish organisational adaptation, leaders need organisational agility. Jack Welch, the former CEO of General Electric, comes to mind when we think about executives who effectively led change via organisational adaptation. An innovator, Jack Welch created trends. He set a good example. He was direct and a brilliant tactician who supported a ruthless method of execution.

Consider Eastman Kodak, a longtime industry leader, which declared bankruptcy in 2012, and Blockbuster Video, which went out of business in 2013. In order to adapt to change, leaders must embrace tools and strategies. Here is a guide to successfully embracing change. Maintain a clear, unwavering vision and communicate it clearly. Establish an organisational culture that is change-friendly. Explain the necessity of change in concrete terms. Inform individuals of the consequences of the status quo. Once the change is in place, show them the advantages. Organise all parties involved efficiently. By allaying their fears, you may remove the obstacles. To guarantee that the full transition occurs easily and without any opposition, demonstrate incremental rewards to them.

In every case, these organisations had shown an exceptional capacity to adjust swiftly to shifting circumstances. These businesses are well positioned to succeed in unpredictable times, with the correct strategy and grit. Many factors will influence an organisation's future health, including changes based on area, industry, and even type. To keep fit while acquiring dynamic competitive advantages, the unifying thread is to focus on revolutionary business drivers. Consider the human dimension while building business models, products, and services for all stakeholders in the organisation.

The vision of the company should be aligned with and served through learning. If you are the CEO of your firm, you must consider yourself the chief learning officer and ask four questions. First, how do your systems enable organisational learning? Second, how can a person communicate with the organisation what they've learnt? Third, how can you use technology to help with learning and knowledge distribution within your organisation? last, what procedures have you put in place to gather and respond to input from both internal and external stakeholders in your organisation?

Finally, feedback-based organisational learning enhances capability. In addition, capacity must be quantified. This means that you must eventually devise a metric for measuring the effectiveness of your capacity in terms of mission enablement. When you work with your executive clients to help them become more adaptable leaders, you start by figuring out who they are—what their personality type is, how they handle stress, how they communicate, what they value, and so on. All of this is in the service of gaining a better understanding of themselves as individuals and then implementing the notion of leadership in light of that knowledge.

For example, Jeff Bezos is well-known for his conviction that meetings centred on PowerPoint did not result in greater capability to carry out their purpose. As a result, he devised the Narrative Meeting Process. He redesigned meetings such that they were focused on a four-to-six-page evidence-based narrative memo that was written before each meeting. He then set aside the first 20 minutes of the meeting to read the material, followed by a substantial discussion and debate in which he questioned the presenting team rigorously. While this change may appear to be logistical or even trivial, it was not. It resulted in the instant sharing of the same. It resulted in an immediate sharing of the same mental model of the situation at hand, resulting in better informed judgments and organisational success.

"The reasonable man adapts himself to the world; the unreasonable one persists in trying to adapt the world to himself. Therefore all progress depends on the unreasonable man." George Bernard Shaw

So, while considering capability, you must consider four factors. First, consider what capabilities and systems are required to assure the success of your mission. Then, consider a team, process, or system in your business and consider how each of these contributes to mission capability. Third, identify how you'll acquire honest criticism that you can use to improve your skills. This is accomplished by linking an organisation's capabilities to its learning systems. Finally, ask yourself how convinced you are that all of your organisation's processes are creating the capability to carry out your purpose.

They have an impact on how individuals interact with one another. Following resilient leadership, these two agenda items should be implemented. The components of culture that substantially impact trust, commitment, motivation, kinship, focus, and social engagement, the traits that constitute psychologically healthy organisations that function at their peak, are added to adaptive corporate culture. Everything in an organisation is influenced by culture. It's just the way things are done here.

Resiliency and toughness in VUCCAD times (volatility, uncertainty, complexity, conflicting, ambiguity, and dynamic settings) were what the COVID-19 crisis best described. In those situations, it was necessary to be able to adjust swiftly to changes, displaying flexibility and agility in combining scheduled tasks with modified ones or completely altering course.

Everywhere in the globe, there is a general air of uncertainty. Everyone faces uncertainty, whether they are leaders or followers, employers or employees. People must have the mentality necessary to accept and cope with uncertainty. To live in the world, they must develop such a mindset and conduct their exploration appropriately. When faced with ambiguity, we must recognise the obstacles that make things difficult for us. We need to consider how damage affects the plans and work we accomplish. To stay on track with our objectives, we must identify the underlying causes of the problems and work toward workable solutions. We must take corrective measures and carefully assess if we were successful in controlling the uncertainty's source.

While fewer limitations could lead to a large number of employees returning to the workplace, this prolonged period of working from home is likely to have long-lasting effects. We anticipated more businesses providing varying degrees of remote work and more flexibility in terms of working hours. After accounting for the gig economy's increasing importance, it is obvious that managing employees will present new difficulties after COVID-19.

At such times, both the business prerequisites and the range of possible business outcomes are subject to rapid change. As a result, communication is thrust to the forefront of operational operations, with the goal of keeping all stakeholders informed. As a result, leaders must communicate effectively with a wide range of goals and target audiences in both internal and external communications. Clear, honest, consistent, dependable, fact-based information is the basic cure for the overwhelming maelstrom of information and changing conditions. Half-truths and reckless optimism have no place when scepticism and worry are pervasive. much less a general lack of knowledge. This necessitates some self-awareness, humility, and receptivity to criticism, as well as a constant stream of verbal and nonverbal communication.

A modified workspace with shared work areas rather than allocated desk spaces or procedures redesigned for remote and hybrid teams are two examples of enabling elements. Overall, this calls for a whole new, more adaptable leadership approach.

Sensitivity and emotional intelligence are necessary to rekindle the passion for everyday operations among stressed, long-isolated employees. People are in need of empathy and understanding after COVID-19, both literally and figuratively speaking. Leaders need to be aware of the longer-term effects of lockdown, including any potential mental health problems or a loss of enthusiasm for the work. Employers may demonstrate empathy by just listening to them with interest. Offering motivation or rewards could be a part of it. In other instances, it can entail suggesting that employees members seek counselling or choosing to adjourn a meeting in order to satisfy employees members' desire for a change of scenery. The ability to mobilise the troops is more probable in the hands of leaders who know how to develop lasting connections with their team members.

Businesses may be tempted to reduce expenditure on leadership development as we have come out of the COVID crisis in an effort to balance the books. However, now more than ever, competent leaders can do their part to help turn the ship in the correct direction. Smaller funds don't have to mean worse development quality when the right priorities are in place. Instead, by releasing our hold on how growth has previously been pursued, we may accept the truth of the present and the future. Rethinking development will require being receptive to many technical approaches and giving soft talents the weight they merit. With new trends emerging to meet changing demands, executive coaching will play an important role in this new environment.

Organisations must be prepared to design people strategies around employee experience and wellness initiatives, use talent corridors to recruit and retain talent, and establish stakeholder trust as the future of technology approaches. Business executives from various sectors will discuss their experiences, the problems and obstacles they encountered during the epidemic, how they all overcame them, and what the future of work holds in order to assist you in achieving your goals.

There is no assurance that the biggest and fiercest industry incumbents will survive as disruption intensifies. Organisations that understand their surroundings and are positioned to detect and respond to change have the best chance of surviving disruptions. Today, no sector or organisation is immune to disruption, yet many companies are ill-equipped to adapt rapidly enough to withstand the consequences of rapid change. Adopting new business sustainability ideas is one way for organisations to start their journey toward becoming more adaptive and, thus, better prepared for an uncertain future.

Any business's primary purpose is to survive and prosper.

The three most frequent strategies employed by individuals to obstruct adaptive change are marginalisation, diversion, and assault. If you observe any of the aforementioned behaviours, your employees may be reluctant to implement the new policy you're trying to implement. The leaders' reluctance to hear what others have to say is maybe the biggest obstacle presented by resilient leadership. Resilient leadership emphasises partnership more than power, as was previously said. Theoretically, resilient leaders should be prepared to pay attention and change suggestions made by subordinates or clients.

However, in practise, only a select few leaders are open to hearing from others who disagree with them. Such leaders misunderstand the fact that listening does not always entail giving up on personal objectives. It simply implies that you are more knowledgeable about the demands of your employees. As a result, you can implement changes more successfully.

Before the pandemic, healthcare was rife with intricate problems and competing objectives that required constant effort to manage ongoing change. It is even more crucial that we try to concentrate and revitalise people now that the public health emergency has hopefully passed and we are beginning to recover. Although leaders may also feel worn out, now is a wonderful moment to be reminded of tried-and-true strategies for maintaining relationships with others and promoting constructive change.

Anyone who had been involved in the healthcare industry in recent past years is aware of how challenging it had been to continually adjust to and deal with the COVID-19 epidemic. These difficulties included several battles on the personal and professional fronts that were made worse by the public health emergency's developing and frequently contentious mitigation measures. It was difficult to navigate what was "normal" prior to COVID-19, though. Physicians, nurses, and other healthcare professionals had long reported high rates of burnout, weariness, and disengagement in the industry. Healthcare administrators struggled with how to effectively fulfil the rising expectations for delivering on the triple aim of excellent treatment, great patient experiences, and economical prices, in addition to growing concerns for employees well-being. These difficulties may have been exacerbated by lingering exhaustion as we work to recover from the COVID-19 epidemic.

Healthcare executives could be more accustomed to servant or transformational leadership philosophies. These models are frequently used to define admirable qualities that uphold the moral principle of helping others while transforming healthcare to better serve patients and communities. Both strategies advocate connecting with people, appealing to common ideals, and imagining bright futures. These admirable attitudes are shared by resilient leadership. Additionally, and maybe more pertinently for navigating the healthcare landscape, resilient leadership places a focus on comprehending the challenges of assisting people in accepting big change and succeeding in facing unsettling facts.

For today's leaders, revitalising their companies could seem like another difficult undertaking. In light of the healthcare industry's fast-paced and complicated dynamics, the key values and practises of resilient leadership can provide a realistic framework for managing big changes while enabling a positive culture that helps engage, empower, and energise physicians and employees.

Given the numerous conflicting challenges, difficult ethical dilemmas, deeply held beliefs, and various cultural norms that can generate conflict and result in unduly stressed physicians and other healthcare professionals, the healthcare setting is ripe with opportunities for applying this approach. Numerous variables affect how people react to change, and what makes someone feel overwhelmed and upset might differ for various people and groups. Resilient leaders are aware of this reality and seek to control the level of suffering in order to prevent unneeded tensions and unhelpful actions.

Many of the components outlined by the Institute of Healthcare Improvement are involved in regulating distress, including clearly outlining why change is necessary, empowering employees to speak up about their priorities, fostering a psychologically safe environment, remaining present and promoting positive engagement, and intervening before tensions reach dangerous levels.

People have a tendency to seek out the comfortable. Changes may cause a great deal of anxiety and distress, especially if they come along with a sense of powerlessness or loss. Tempering the timing of new initiatives is an excellent example of how to control stress in healthcare companies. This involves purposefully avoiding the deployment of too many changes at once and making sure to complete ongoing projects before starting the next significant endeavour.

Helping clinical employees comprehend the realities of increasingly problematic payment arrangements and the necessity to embrace new strategies for providing treatment that is both cost-effective and safe are examples of compassionate but disciplined attention. To balance this, it is important to acknowledge that too much focus on the numbers might give the impression that administrators and practitioners care more about margins than patients, which runs counter to the previous three principles.

For instance, advising doctors that they must go above and beyond to reach a new quality target may frequently encounter strong opposition and conflict. Positive ideas and workable solutions are far more likely to be generated when the background is explained, the significance is communicated, and the audience is asked for suggestions on how to assess and accomplish a quality target. Applying the first four resilient leadership concepts effectively creates a strong basis for giving back to individuals on the front lines, empowering them, and allowing them to thrive.

On a fundamental level, this element has to do with ensuring that leaders stay receptive to suggestions from all organisational levels. This comprises those who hold opposing or minoritarian viewpoints. When faced with difficult circumstances and when group consensus might not be supportive of opposing viewpoints, this can be a particularly difficult task. Additionally, there could be a delicate balance between encouraging acceptance of all viewpoints and the requirement to occasionally moderate disruptive debate. However, being open to many approaches to problems can result in creative solutions that might not otherwise be found. Additionally, it prevents groupthink, which may restrict original thought, obscure fresh perspectives, and undermine the ability to make wise decisions.

Using interdisciplinary teams with members from various departments coming together to share their views and provide ideas on how to best improve processes while meeting standards for quality, patient experience, costs, and, perhaps most importantly, maintaining a positive culture, is a good example of enabling input from all levels in healthcare.

Engaging people, helping teams, and inspiring others to accomplish goals are all important components of the modern servant, transformational, and resilient leadership paradigms. However, given the rate and scope of change in healthcare, the resilient model may be particularly pertinent and useful in evaluating these and other widely accepted leadership theories. The values and practises of resilient leadership may help to refocus efforts, engage, empower, and motivate doctors, nurses, and the many other dedicated people who are involved in giving their patients and communities safe and effective care.

Recent financial crises have demonstrated the necessity for businesses to develop more reliable business models. However, it appears that most managers don't prioritise building resilience until after a shock of this nature has already occurred. Resilience refers to a organisation's capacity to adapt, endure, recover, and eventually prosper despite the shock. Managers may explicitly choose actions that will strengthen their organisation's resilience, boosting their chances of predicting and avoiding these shocks through responsible leadership. This book, which is the outcome of a three-years study effort spanning multiple sectors, aims to increase knowledge of why some businesses are more adept at navigating market turmoil than others.

To create a metric for organisational resilience, highlighting its factors and showing how businesses may benefit from high resilience levels. For graduates completing a course in strategy and worldwide management as well as for self-reflective practitioners, it is a worthwhile read. "Be strong and upbeat." What does today's leader successfully do to guide his team to success if the COVID-19 pandemic alters the way we think? This and other concerns are addressed in "Key Post-Pandemic Business Resilient Leadership." What factors enable a resilient business to achieve remarkable performance in the post-pandemic environment? Last but not least, do you want to make a positive contribution today if the survival of the planet is in our hand? we won't succumb before the changes because all human beings are inherently resilient and building resilience is also imperative? Where do we find the pertinent knowledge we need to practise resilient, constructive leadership in the modern era? What are the most significant benefits of fostering resilience inside our organisation?

Organisations must exhibit a resilient edge on a regular basis.

Leaders must pay immediate attention to the aftermath of the pandemic problem, not just for present employees but also for new generations joining the workforce. Younger people are increasingly pressuring their employers to change their business models from linear to circular. If leaders do not respond in a comprehensive and constructive manner, they risk losing a whole generation of engaged brains who will gladly contemplate taking their skills elsewhere.

Communication is one of the most significant problems of the hybrid work paradigm, and it has resulted in a trust gap between employees and supervisors. While trust is important in all relationships, it is especially important in the workplace. As a result of the new hybrid working style, employees are reevaluating their relationships with their employers. If leadership does not respond to this new reality, there is a significant danger of trust breakdown and attrition.

Resilient Leadership looks at business challenges through a fresh perspective, challenging standard leadership approaches that have reigned in businesses for years. Resilient leaders can create dynamic teams that embrace change and convert uncertainty into opportunities. While some people are born with the ability to alter leadership styles, others must learn and practice the behaviors of great adaptable leaders.

No one is an island, and organisations and the individuals who work in them are no different. Authenticity improves a leader's relatability, humility, and ability to evolve in step with the demands of their business. Resilient leaders display vulnerability and compassion instead of actively boosting their perceived authority in times of uncertainty, providing psychological safety for their team members to do the same. When people feel secure being themselves and taking risks, their performance rises. Because all three are basic psychological needs, their performance is likely to increase even more if colleagues' needs to feel competent, linked, and autonomous are acknowledged, understood, and met.

"Adaptability is not imitation. It means the power of resistance and assimilation."- Mahatma Gandhi

It's never been more crucial to provide people and teams with the tools they need to succeed—to reach their full potential and optimise their skills. Organisations may increase their paths to success by identifying leadership as a characteristic existing in everyone of us rather than a duty for one individual to fulfill. One individual cannot possibly possess the depth and breadth of talent, knowledge, or insight required to navigate our rapidly changing future—and there is no expectation that they will under resilient leadership. Resilient leadership uses its collective spirit to create internal and external networks, collaborations, and interactions.

Finding and pursuing a greater purpose becomes even more important in uncertain times. A common purpose, backed by a set of shared values, may assist companies enhance focus, cohesiveness, and resilience. When team members are connected, working toward the same goal, and confident in their organisation's cohesive thinking, they are more likely to tackle complicated challenges together. A clear shared purpose and values may comfort employees about an organisation's overarching objective, instill a feeling of ownership across its teams, and, as a result, inspire better performance.

Leadership in the future will not be "one size fits all." Organisations must be prepared to adapt, bend, learn, and listen as the rate of change continues to accelerate. Leaders must understand the requirements of their employees, customers, markets, and the environment in order to lead in ways that meet, surpass, and harmonize with ever-changing expectations.

You seek to provide businesses and leaders with clarity on resilient leadership as well as the skills to fully embrace future change. You assist them in incorporating environmental, social, and governance factors into their operational models. You could rely on the stable assumption that the present and future will in some ways mimic the past in periods of slower change. This type of linear thinking lacks the breadth and depth required to navigate the future, let alone guide others through it.

If the appropriate conditions for personal learning are in place, leaders can enhance their resiliency. A powerful learning process is created when challenging assignments are joined with opportunities to reflect with people who are willing and able to provide honest and constructive feedback, coaching, and support.

Individuals and organisations can discover how to strengthen the critical executive capability of adaptability through a continuous learning culture. Opportunities for assessment, practice of new behaviors in conjunction with ongoing support and encouragement, timely feedback, and rewards for the development and execution of innovation and business performance improvement are all part of successful leadership and organisational development strategies.

Resilient leadership is greeted with a lot of opposition and requires a lot of effort, but the outcomes are well worth it. Organisations that adopt resilient leadership reap considerable financial and operational benefits. When everyone's talents and abilities are utilised as part of a team effort, it leads to more pleasant working conditions, greater intra-team bonds, and healthier client connections.

Individuals who rely on a short-term fix to meet a specific demand may be able to survive for the time being. However, in order to achieve long-term success and development, organisations must continue to change—quickly and at scale—in order to fulfill larger market and consumer expectations. Businesses that are really adaptable are those that understand their consumers, conduct trials, and focus on achieving outsised results. Finally, despite excellent intentions, businesses confront a variety of problems in implementing their plans and meeting their goals, including a lack of customer awareness owing to disconnected data and increased consumer expectations for better digital experiences.

Leading organisations must exhibit an adaptable edge and update their business strategy on a regular basis. How do critical organisations create resilient advantage at the most fundamental level? Building technology-base resilient advantage successful species in biological ecosystems that are subject to extremely dynamic conditions are those that can adapt. Rapid adaptation necessitates creatures seeing more, thinking quicker, and reacting socially in their environment. Increasing the competitiveness of technology transformation companies are investing in technological efforts in order to develop new business models and increase efficiency. Without a doubt, technology has aided in the formation of some of the world's most profitable corporations.

In this traditional system, the highest layer of management is normally responsible for identifying the proper answers. The top layer of management is frequently viewed as a single entity that will give order, direction, and protection. Order, direction, and protection are all crucial characteristics of leadership, but they do not define it. Someone who can lead people through resilient changes is referred to as a leader. Leadership is not guided by a single person, but by a group of people working together to achieve a common purpose. When confronted with a problem for which there is no one-size-fits-all solution, resilient leadership becomes critical.

Keeping an eye on your rival is unavoidable. You must actively research how well they are responding to change, as well as how far behind or ahead of them you are. Business leaders must prioritise and encourage flexibility as a must-have organisational quality if they want to position themselves for long-term success in an ever-changing market. Traditional metrics of corporate health are no longer sufficient. To become resilient now and survive tomorrow, the focus must be on shifting viewpoints and morphing swiftly and at scale.

The way things are done in a organisation reflects the habits and attitudes of its employees. It is an organisation's "secret sauce," bringing a plan to life or killing it. Culture is not set in stone. Cultivating a distinct culture is both achievable and important. Employee engagement, on the other hand, is defined as employees' desire to go above and beyond for a organisation, not only out of responsibility or for monetary gain, but because work is important to them personally and professionally.

Culture helps achieve strategic goals faster.

Leadership, design, people, and change management are not the same as culture and engagement; culture and engagement are results of the other traits. In the same way that people strengthen their hearts by exercising other bodily muscles, organisations enhance culture and engagement indirectly by working on other traits. Performance management systems, for example, which are part of the people dimension, may have a significant influence on culture. A good organisational culture does not happen by chance. To accomplish strategic goals, high-performance businesses establish, maintain, and monitor a culture. A risk-averse, process-oriented culture with clear lines of authority may be perfectly logical for an airline, but it's a formula for poor performance in an Internet corporation. At each particular time, a organisation's culture either works or doesn't work for a certain organisation. Culture should evolve in tandem with strategic aims.

A good organisational culture does not happen by chance. To accomplish strategic goals, high-performance businesses establish, maintain, and monitor a culture. A risk-averse, process-oriented culture with clear lines of authority may be perfectly logical for an airline, but it's a formula for poor performance in an Internet corporation. At each particular time, a organisation's culture either works or doesn't work for a certain organisation.

Culture should evolve in tandem with strategic aims. Personal motivators, like recognition, and performance disciplines, such as performance management measures, are at the core of employee engagement. High-performance organisations keep an eye on their employees' pulses, assessing engagement levels on a regular basis and actively managing engagement during challenging periods like restructuring or large-scale change initiatives.

Organisations frequently make changes to their

organisation and people aspects in response to external events, hiring more people during good times, laying off employees during bad times, and then offering leadership training when morale eventually drops and the organisation experiences whiplash reactions. Others have a more laid-back style with few proactive measures. Neither of these procedures produces consistently good results.

Organisations with high performance just operate differently. They recognise the importance of having all traits in their organisation and work together to put them in place. They also determine which of the trait is the most important for long-term competitive advantage and strive to strengthen weak areas through a systematic set of initiatives and activities.

Furthermore, successful organisations regularly monitor and measure their adherence to these traits with the same zeal and expertise they demand of themselves in terms of financial and operational performance. The search for the optimal organisational and human traits is no longer a black box. Just as the introduction of MRI technology gave doctors a previously inaccessible visual depiction of organs and muscles, this framework provides businesses a window into previously unknown internal dynamics, and access to this information may lead to sustained performance.

Does your company's culture value and promote learning from mistakes?

A culture is made up of several components, all of which contribute to the tone, mood, and expectations that surround the workforce and impact their attitude and approach to work. A resilient corporate culture (adaptive culture) is one that is purposefully developed to generate the tone, mood, and expectations of a psychologically healthy organisation, one that encourages employees to feel good.

The idea is that the organisation would reach peak performance through improving the psychological well-being of its employees. As a result, the culture must contain triggers that cause people to act in specific ways and feel accountable for the organisation's future success. Purpose, vision, cultural values, business values, and architecture are the key causes.

"The greatest approach to inspiring invention is to foster a culture of thanks and appreciation."

A resilient corporate culture enables a organisation to respond swiftly and effectively to internal and external change demands. A business culture that continuously promotes a healthy psychological environment will make employees more stress-resistant. Such a workforce will be able to adjust to change successfully while maintaining productivity. Any organisation using the methods detailed in the WellBeing and performance agenda must adopt the concepts of adaptive leadership as a top priority, and no change in attitude or practice will occur until someone or several individuals take the initiative. Two elements that underpin the culture of the organisation are psychological responsibility and sharing responsibility for the organisation's future success.

Culture also affects the organisation's health.

Is it possible for CEOs to take frequent breaks from activity to find time for reflection and renewal? These are some of the questions that organizations that seek to promote executive flexibility should ask. Organisations will be able to build the leadership talent needed to effectively handle significant strategic problems if these questions are well addressed. Individual and organizational performance will soar to new heights as a result of adaptable leadership.

The corporate culture has been engrained with a lack of accountability and a tendency to blame others for missed deadlines. The HR personnel, as well as the team managers, were part of the problem. To transform the culture, input from the whole organisation was solicited. Clearly, there were difficulties and disagreements during the process, and suggested modifications were greeted with opposition from many in top-tier management and teams across many departments. Instead, businesses must figure out how teams naturally connect with one another and with customers, and then create multidisciplinary teams, communities, reporting relationships, and communication channels to enable such interactions.

If you want to overcome this challenge as an adaptable leader, you'll need to enlist the help of the whole organisation in transforming the culture. As a result of this process, there will almost certainly be a lot of awkward conversations, disagreements, and roadblocks. You'll have to give the leadership team difficult feedback while also being open to receiving it yourself. It's possible that you'll have to cope with your own anxieties and disappointments. It will take time for the shift to take hold, and it will almost certainly be greeted with resistance from a variety of sources.

Change is a methodical process.

However, you will only be able to effectively solve this difficulty if you go through this procedure. Despite the high failure rate of change initiatives, a few organisations are succeeding. They make certain that the leadership team is on the same page about the organisation's goals and strategies for change, and they intentionally convey that alignment to employees layer by layer throughout the organisation. Senior executives receive feedback from deep inside the business, where the destiny of the change is decided, in order to track progress and make modifications during a large transition. This is known as cascading change. Organisations achieve minimal sufficiency by focusing on the most crucial parts of cascading change and doing just enough to succeed without fragmenting focus and effort needlessly.

Organisations that do so use both hard and soft techniques to bring about change. Individual accountability and metrics are defined, and individuals are given the tools and power they need to succeed in implementation. They keep track of their progress against key milestones, recognise when projects are running late, and take remedial action. In order to preserve trust, they also interact and engage with important stakeholders.

Organisations with lean architecture may focus on meaningful work rather than coordinating. Activities that do not provide value are removed. Communication and decision-making are faster with fewer organisational levels, and senior executives have a clearer picture of day-to-day operations and consumer interactions. Managers become more ambitious in using their leadership talents as their spans of influence become larger. They don't have time to micromanage, but they may gain confidence in their leadership, coaching, and inspiring abilities. Although lean organisations have a reduced cost base, the additional benefits of success outweigh the financial ones.

High-performance organisations have clearly defined responsibilities that are meticulously put together to make a highly efficient organisation. People are aware of what is expected of them and which decisions they have control over. Employees understand when and with whom they must cooperate when accountability is shared. Role charters are one way we help organisations achieve this clarity, but the name is less essential than having a route to explicit accountability, decision rights, and behavioral requirements. Clear roles eliminate the uncertainty that hinders decision-making and boost modern businesses' performance potential and employee engagement. Peers in a organisation can use role charters to have open and honest discussions about individual, collective, and shared responsibilities.

While many businesses excel in recruitment, training, or performance management, high-performance organisations excel at translating their organisation plan into a compelling people strategy. HR serves as a key advisor to business units on both operational and strategic people concerns in these businesses. It includes short- and long-term strategies for attracting, developing, and keeping the best individuals with the best skills.

A key asset is the employer brand.

Employer brands are well-defined in high-performance organisations. Employees and recruits alike are aware of the wide variety of perks available to them, including professional growth, job rotation, and prestige, as well as flexibility and autonomy. This brand—or employee value proposition—contributes to a organisation's competitive advantage and strengths. Employee development is prioritised in high-performance organisations, which invest in training and rotation of jobs and responsibilities. These encounters may beat remuneration and other financial incentives as a significant motivator and retention strategy. They also promote teamwork and decrease the chances of localised leadership. By the time they reach the upper echelons, employees have a comprehensive view of the organisation.

Organisational design requires compromise. A well-designed structure should stress the most important aspects of a organisation. It is difficult to accommodate all dimensions evenly in the real world. For example, a corporation concentrating on future success in major markets can arrange its operations by area rather than channel. Even while channels did not represent the main axis in the organisation, its leaders would need to make cautious efforts to guarantee that they were receiving sufficient support. The structure of an organisation should also be dynamic, focusing on current and future objectives rather than legacy priorities. An organisation's structure may need to be adjusted as strategy, performance, or the competitive environment change.

One of resilient leadership's strengths is also one of its limitations. For the most part, an adaptable leader must place less value on structure in order to efficiently execute change. Some employees, on the other hand, thrive in regimented workplaces, and resilient leadership would be a poor match for them. An adaptable leader will attempt to provide some structure for those employees that require it. Nonetheless, in this unstructured work environment, there are still possibilities for individuals to be less productive. It's in the nature of rules to be broken. An ethical leader may squirm after seeing how an adaptable leader operates. Ethical leaders support an organization's policies because they correspond with their own personal beliefs. An adaptable leader, on the other hand, may bend (or even break) the laws within the bounds of the law in order for the business to undertake the most effective change plan feasible.

Resilient leaders are always looking for new methods to match pivotal events with shifting consumer preferences. They are attempting to alter client preferences in ways that benefit both their companies and their customers. They train their employees for both expected and unexpected outcomes. They can feel when things are about to change and react rapidly. These adaptable leaders are able to function effectively, adapt rapidly, invent new methods of working, and alter their businesses in a seamless manner. Organisations must produce leaders who can adjust themselves and their organisations to deal with challenges now.

Describe the technical and interpersonal skills you've developed as a result of your leadership development. Ensure that articulated purpose and talent management executives are enabled by competences. Explain the stages of leadership competency for different types of leaders, such as individual contributors, subject matter experts, project managers, executives, people leaders, high performers, and emerging executives. Incorporate expected outcome delivery into recruiting, onboarding, learning and development, and performance management methods. Ensure that thought leaders‘ leadership approaches are tailored to your organisation's goals.

Resilient leaders are always looking for new methods to match pivotal events with shifting consumer preferences. They are attempting to alter client preferences in ways that benefit both their companies and their customers. They train their employees for both expected and unexpected outcomes. They can feel when things are about to change and react rapidly. These adaptable leaders are able to function effectively, adapt rapidly, invent new methods of working, and alter their businesses in a seamless manner. Organisations must produce leaders who can adjust themselves and their organisations to deal with challenges now.

Finally, change may be frightening, disturbing, and disconcerting. Fear, tension, resentment, and resistance can arise even when change is anticipated or desired. These reactions to change are frequently perceived by leaders as a hurdle that must be overcome. Resilient leaders must be able to determine when to enter the conflict and when to exit and observe from the sidelines.

Leadership barriers to resilient capacity changing one's conduct in reaction to adversity does not come easily for many business executives. While most business executives are competent and clever, it can be challenging to acquire new behavioral reactions when their previous habits match their businesses' goals in the majority of circumstances. Introducing new behavioral options is typically unsettling, and it may make leaders feel exposed. People tend to cling to practices that have served them well in the past, which might limit their ability to change. Rather than waiting for agility to spread from the bottom up, HR executives must support and assist leaders in taking command of their transitions. These techniques can aid in the development of an adaptable leadership style.

A culture that encourages individuals to feel psychologically good while also motivating them to achieve peak performance motivates them to be extremely successful. As a consequence, dedication, trust, motivation, kinship, focus, and social involvement characterise the organisation and workforce. These are the characteristics and behaviors that make businesses so successful.

About The Author

Dr. Amit Das, is a renowned executive advisor, consultant, educationist, author, speaker, counsellor, and coach whose 25+ years of business experience provides high-impact, practical solutions that support his clients' leadership development and organisational transformations. He worked for fortune 500 companies and left rich leagacy of organising transformational learning workshops. He has transformed more than 5000+ working executives through his path breaking capability building learning workshops. Dr. Amit Das is recognised as an innovative, principled thought leader who combines intellectual rigor and discipline with an ability to translate theory into practice. His operational skills are coupled with a strategic ability to analyse, develop, and implement successful strategies for profitability, growth, and sustainability.

Dr. Amit Das has a successful track record in aligning learning and training solutions to key business strategy with a strong focus on flawless execution excellence to facilitate individual, business divisional, and organisational performance. He keeps relentless focus on measuring training impact and ROI, people capability building graphs, training process governance, performance coaching, and strategic thinking. These have been some of his key individual success traits. His core capabilities include performance coaching, designing training and development frameworks, psychometric assessment and analysis, competency framework development and assessments, content design and facilitation of soft skills and leadership programmes, Learning Management Systems, Learning Impact Measurement, Talent Analysis, and Performance Coaching and Counselling.

Dr. Amit Das has authored multiple management and self-development books, like Redefining Organisational Excellence, High Impact Leadership, Redefining Corporate Spectrum, Create Your Leadership Edge, Love-Laugh- Live With Happiness, SMART Parenting @ Zero Cost, Redefining HRM, Building Organisational Capability, Ethical Road Map, Attomic Attention, BYPB, Redefining The Power Of Mentoring, Making The Most Future Fit Organisation, Redefining Talent Management, Defining Your Success Factors, Lead or Plead, Make The Most Of Your Life, Better Half or Bitter Half, Psychology Of Learning And Development, The Transformative Mind & Soul are few of them.

He has a Ph.D. and a Fellowship in strategic learning, along with his first class degrees in Human Resource Management, Marketing Management, International Business, and Corporate Laws from the top business schools in India. He is a certified Psychometric analyst, HR Analyst, OD Interventionist, Human Psychologist, Lifecoach, Leadership Developer, Black Belt (LSS), Strategic Thinker, Talent Analyst, certified professional trainer from the U.K. and certified behavioral coach from the U.S.A.

Dr. Amit Das likes googling, reading books, writing articles & books, cooking, listening to old melodies, and counselling people to unleash their true potential to build a strong nation. He is married and blessed with a son. He would love to hear about your experience after reading his books. You can email him and share your thoughts, or you can use his services for life coaching, positive behavioural counseling, educational support, and mentoring for young, promising students pursuing their B.B.A. and M.B.A. degrees.

References

- *Leverage Leadership: A Practical Guide to Building Exceptional Schools (Paperback) by Doug Lemov, published 2012*
- *Rethinking Leadership: A Collection of Articles (Paperback) by Thomas J. Sergiovanni (Editor), published 1999*
- *Leadership on the Line, With a New Preface: Staying Alive Through the Dangers of Change (Kindle Edition) by Ronald A. Heifetz*
- *We Want to Do More Than Survive: Abolitionist Teaching and the Pursuit of Educational Freedom (Hardcover) by Bettina L. Love, published 2019*
- *Solving Tough Problems: An Open Way of Talking, Listening, and Creating New Realities (Hardcover) by Adam Kahane (Goodreads Author), published 2004*
- *Change the World: How Ordinary People Can Accomplish Extraordinary Things (Hardcover) by Robert E. Quinn (Goodreads Author), published 2000*
- *Practical Approaches to Marketing Analytics in the Digital Age (ebook) by Cesar A. Brea, published 2012*
- *Resilient Leadership 2.0: Leading with Calm, Clarity, and Conviction in Anxious Times Kindle Edition by Bob Duggan (Author), Bridgette Theurer (Author), Dec 2017.*
- *Resilient Leadership: Beyond myths and misunderstandings Paperback – Import, 30 September 2020 by Karsten Drath.*
- *The Innovative University: Changing the DNA of Higher Education from the Inside Out (Hardcover)by Clayton M. Christensen, published 2011*

- *Reinventing Higher Education: The Promise of Innovation (Hardcover) by Ben Wildavsky (Editor), published 2011*
- *Bass & Stogdill's Handbook of Leadership: Theory, Research & Managerial Applications (Hardcover) by Bernard M. Bass, published 1990*
- *The practice of Adaptive Leadership: Tools and Tactics for Changing Your Organization and the world (Hardcover) by Ronald A. Heifetz, published 2009*
- *The Third Side: Why We Fight and How We Can Stop (Paperback) by William Ury, published 2000*
- *Accelerate: Building Strategic Agility for a Faster-Moving World (Hardcover) by John P. Kotter (Goodreads Author), published 2012*
- *How Colleges Change: Understanding, Leading, and Enacting Change (ebook) by Adrianna Kezar, published 2013*
- *Adaptation Studies and Learning: New Frontiers (Paperback) by Laurence Raw, published 2013*
- *More Than 50 Ways to Build Team Consensus (Paperback) by R. Bruce Williams, published 1993*
- *Adaptability: Responding Effectively to Change (Paperback) by Allan Calarco, published 2006*
- *Building Resiliency: How to Thrive in Times of Change (Paperback) by Mary Lynn Pulley, published 2001*
- *Resilient Leadership: Navigating the Hidden Chemistry of Organizations Kindle Edition by Bob Duggan (Author), Jim Moyer (Author), Dec 2020.*
- *Resilient Leadership for Turbulent Times: A Guide to Thriving in the Face of Adversity Paperback – Import, 16 March 2010 by Jerry L. Patterson (Author), George A. Goens (Author), Diane E. Reed (Author).*
- *Playing to Win: How Strategy Really Works (Hardcover) by A.G. Lafley, published 2013*

- *Leadership Without Easy Answers (Hardcover) by Ronald A. Heifetz, published 1994*
- *Influencer: The Power to Change Anything (Hardcover) by Kerry Patterson, published 2007*
- *Leadership on the Line: Staying Alive Through the Dangers of Leading (Hardcover)by Ronald A. Heifetz , published 2002*
- *Leading for Powerful Learning: A Guide for Instructional Leaders (Paperback) by Angela Breidenstein, published 2012*
- *Theory U: Leading from the Future as it Emerges (Hardcover) by C. Otto Scharmer (Goodreads Author), published 2007*
- *Executive Advantage: Resilient Leadership for 21st-Century Organizations Paperback – 3 February 2013 by Jacqui Grey (Author).*
- *Resilient Organizations: Responsible Leadership in Times of Uncertainty Hardcover – Import, 22 December 2016 by Guia Beatrice Pirotti (Author), Markus Venzin (Author).*
- *Complex Adaptive Leadership: Embracing Paradox and Uncertainty (Hardcover) by Nick Obolensky, published 2000*
- *Invaluable Master the 10 Skills You Need to Skyrocket Your Career by Maya Grossman, published 2020|*
- *Invaluable, Master the 10 Skills You Need to Skyrocket Your Career by Maya Grossman, published 2020*
- *The Effective Executive , The Definitive Guide to Getting the Right Things Done by Peter F. Drucker, Zachary First, Jim Collins, publish 2017*
- *The Leadership Challenge, How to Make Extraordinary Things Happen in Organizations by James M. Kouzes, Barry Z. Posner, published 2017*
- *Multipliers, How the Best Leaders Make Everyone Smarter*

by Liz Wiseman, Greg McKeown, published 2014

- *The Leadership Gap, What Gets Between You and Your Greatness by Lolly Daskal, published 2017*
- *Be Resilient Positive: Key to post-pandemic business resilient leadership, Kindle edition by Edgar Eduardo Romero Martinez (author), Jan 2021.*
- *Reset for Resilience: Developing a Resilient Enterprise to Thrive in a Never Normal World Paperback – Import, 30 October 2021 by Antonio Urquiza (Author), Marcelo Sauro (Contributor).*
- *The Power of Positive Leadership, How and Why Positive Leaders Transform Teams and Organizations and Change the World by Jon Gordon, published 2017*
- *Wooden on Leadership, How to Create a Winning Organization by John Wooden, Steve Jamison, published 2005*
- *Learning Leadership, The Five Fundamentals of Becoming an Exemplary Leader by James M. Kouzes, Barry Z. Posner, published 2016*
- *5 Levels of Leadership, Proven Steps to Maximize Your Potential by John C. Maxwell, published 2013*
- *Real Leadership, 9 Simple Practices for Leading and Living with Purpose by John Addison, John David Mann, published|2016*
- *TouchPoints, Creating Powerful Leadership Connections in the Smallest of Moments by Douglas Conant, Mette Norgaard, published 2011*
- *Organizational Culture and Leadership by Edgar H. Schein, published 2010*
- *The Practice of Adaptive Leadership, Tools and Tactics for Changing Your Organization and the World by Ronald A. Heifetz, Marty Linsky, Alexander Grashow, published 2009*

- *Leadership: Theory and practice. Los Angeles, CA: SAGE Publications, Inc by Northouse, P. published 2019*
- *All Systems Go: The Change Imperative for Whole System Reform (Paperback)by Michael Fullan, published 2010*
- *The Constructivist Leader (Paperback) by Deborah Walker,published 1995*
- *Credibility: How Leaders Gain and Lose It, Why People Demand It (Paperback) by James M. Kouzes, published 1993*
- *Appreciative Leadership: Focus on What Works to Drive Winning Performance and Build a Thriving Organization (Hardcover) by Diana Whitney, published 2010*
- *Thinking, Fast and Slow (Hardcover) by Daniel Kahneman, published 2011*
- *The Checklist Manifesto: How to Get Things Right (Hardcover) by Atul Gawande, published 2009*
- *The Heart of Change: Real-Life Stories of How People Change Their Organizations (Hardcover) by John P. Kotter (Goodreads Author), published 2002*
- *Harvard Business Review on Leading Through Change (Paperback) by Harvard Business School Press (Compilation), published 2006*
- *Boards That Lead: When to Take Charge, When to Partner, and When to Stay Out of the Way (Hardcover) by Ram Charan, published 2013*
- *Innovation in the Schoolhouse: Entrepreneurial Leadership in Education (ebook)by Jack Leonard, published 2013*
- *Chaos, Complexity and Leadership 2012 (Hardcover) by Santo Banerjee (Editor), published 2013*
- *Checklist for Change: Making American Higher Education a Sustainable Enterprise (Hardcover)by Robert Zemsky, published 2013*
- *Nudge: Improving Decisions About Health, Wealth, and*

Happiness (Paperback) by Richard H. Thaler, published 2008

- *Leadership 2050: Critical Challenges, Key Contexts and Emerging Trends (Building Leadership Bridges) Paperback – July 24, 2015 by Matthew Sowcik (Author).*
- *2030: How Today's Biggest Trends Will Collide and Reshape the Future of Everything Hardcover – 25 August 2020 by Mauro F. Guillen (Author).*
- *Future Fit: How to Stay Relevant and Competitive in the Future of Work Paperback – Import, 25 May 2021 by Andrea Clarke (Author).*
- *Made in Future: A Story of Marketing, Media, and Content for our Times Hardcover – Import, 16 May 2022 by Prashant Kumar (Author).*
- *The Future Is Faster Than You Think Paperback – 17 February 2020 by Peter H. Diamandis and Steven Kotler (Author).*
- *Leadership: Theory and practice. Los Angeles, CA: SAGE Publications, Inc by Northouse, P. published 2019.*
- *All Systems Go: The Change Imperative for Whole System Reform (Paperback)by Michael Fullan, published 2010.*
- *The Constructivist Leader (Paperback) by Deborah Walker,published 1995.*
- *Credibility: How Leaders Gain and Lose It, Why People Demand It (Paperback) by James M. Kouzes, published 1993.*
- *Appreciative Leadership: Focus on What Works to Drive Winning Performance and Build a Thriving Organization (Hardcover) by Diana Whitney, published 2010.*
- *Thinking, Fast and Slow (Hardcover) by Daniel Kahneman, published 2011.*
- *The Checklist Manifesto: How to Get Things Right (Hardcover) by Atul Gawande, published 2009.*

- *The Heart of Change: Real-Life Stories of How People Change Their Organizations (Hardcover) by John P. Kotter (Goodreads Author), published 2002.*
- *Harvard Business Review on Leading Through Change (Paperback) by Harvard Business School Press (Compilation), published 2006.*
- *Boards That Lead: When to Take Charge, When to Partner, and When to Stay Out of the Way (Hardcover) by Ram Charan, published 2013.*
- *Innovation in the Schoolhouse: Entrepreneurial Leadership in Education (ebook)by Jack Leonard, published 2013.*
- *Chaos, Complexity and Leadership 2012 (Hardcover) by Santo Banerjee (Editor), published 2013.*
- *Checklist for Change: Making American Higher Education a Sustainable Enterprise (Hardcover)by Robert Zemsky, published 2013.*
- *Nudge: Improving Decisions About Health, Wealth, and Happiness (Paperback) by Richard H. Thaler, published 2008.*
- *Leverage Leadership: A Practical Guide to Building Exceptional Schools (Paperback) by Doug Lemov, published 2012.*
- *Rethinking Leadership: A Collection of Articles (Paperback) by Thomas J. Sergiovanni (Editor), published 1999.*
- *Leadership on the Line, With a New Preface: Staying Alive Through the Dangers of Change (Kindle Edition) by Ronald A. Heifetz.*
- *We Want to Do More Than Survive: Abolitionist Teaching and the Pursuit of Educational Freedom (Hardcover) by Bettina L. Love, published 2019.*
- *Solving Tough Problems: An Open Way of Talking, Listening, and Creating New Realities (Hardcover) by*

Adam Kahane (Goodreads Author), published 2004.

- *Change the World: How Ordinary People Can Accomplish Extraordinary Things (Hardcover) by Robert E. Quinn (Goodreads Author), published 2000.*
- *Practical Approaches to Marketing Analytics in the Digital Age (ebook) by Cesar A. Brea, published 2012.*
- *The Innovative University: Changing the DNA of Higher Education from the Inside Out (Hardcover)by Clayton M. Christensen, published 2011.*
- *Reinventing Higher Education: The Promise of Innovation (Hardcover) by Ben Wildavsky (Editor), published 2011.*
- *Bass & Stogdill's Handbook of Leadership: Theory, Research & Managerial Applications (Hardcover) by Bernard M. Bass, published 1990.*
- *The practice of Adaptive Leadership: Tools and Tactics for Changing Your Organization and the world (Hardcover) by Ronald A. Heifetz, published 2009.*
- *The Third Side: Why We Fight and How We Can Stop (Paperback) by William Ury, published 2000.*
- *Accelerate: Building Strategic Agility for a Faster-Moving World (Hardcover) by John P. Kotter (Goodreads Author), published 2012.*
- *How Colleges Change: Understanding, Leading, and Enacting Change (ebook) by Adrianna Kezar, published 2013.*
- *Adaptation Studies and Learning: New Frontiers (Paperback) by Laurence Raw, published 2013*
- *More Than 50 Ways to Build Team Consensus (Paperback) by R. Bruce Williams, published 1993.*
- *Adaptability: Responding Effectively to Change (Paperback) by Allan Calarco, published 2006*
- *Building Resiliency: How to Thrive in Times of Change (Paperback) by Mary Lynn Pulley, published 2001.*

- *Playing to Win: How Strategy Really Works (Hardcover) by A.G. Lafley, published 2013*
- *Leadership Without Easy Answers (Hardcover) by Ronald A. Heifetz, published 1994.*
- *Influencer: The Power to Change Anything (Hardcover) by Kerry Patterson, published 2007*
- *Leadership on the Line: Staying Alive Through the Dangers of Leading (Hardcover)by Ronald A. Heifetz , published 2002.*
- *Leading for Powerful Learning: A Guide for Instructional Leaders (Paperback) by Angela Breidenstein, published 2012.*
- *Theory U: Leading from the Future as it Emerges (Hardcover) by C. Otto Scharmer (Goodreads Author), published 2007.*
- *Complex Adaptive Leadership: Embracing Paradox and Uncertainty (Hardcover) by Nick Obolensky, published 2000.*
- *Invaluable Master the 10 Skills You Need to Skyrocket Your Career by Maya Grossman, published 2020.*
- *Invaluable, Master the 10 Skills You Need to Skyrocket Your Career by Maya Grossman, published 2020.*
- *The Effective Executive , The Definitive Guide to Getting the Right Things Done by Peter F. Drucker, Zachary First, Jim Collins, publish 2017.*
- *The Leadership Challenge, How to Make Extraordinary Things Happen in Organizations by James M. Kouzes, Barry Z. Posner, published 2017.*
- *Multipliers, How the Best Leaders Make Everyone Smarter by Liz Wiseman, Greg McKeown, published 2014.*
- *The Leadership Gap, What Gets Between You and Your Greatness by Lolly Daskal, published 2017.*
- *The Power of Positive Leadership, How and Why Positive*

Leaders Transform Teams and Organizations and Change the World by Jon Gordon, published 2017.

- *Wooden on Leadership, How to Create a Winning Organization by John Wooden, Steve Jamison, published 2005.*
- *Learning Leadership, The Five Fundamentals of Becoming an Exemplary Leader by James M. Kouzes, Barry Z. Posner, published 2016.*
- *5 Levels of Leadership, Proven Steps to Maximize Your Potential by John C. Maxwell, published 2013.*
- *Real Leadership, 9 Simple Practices for Leading and Living with Purpose by John Addison, John David Mann, published in 2016.*
- *TouchPoints, Creating Powerful Leadership Connections in the Smallest of Moments by Douglas Conant, Mette Norgaard, published 2011.*
- *Organizational Culture and Leadership by Edgar H. Schein, published 2010.*
- *The Practice of Adaptive Leadership, Tools and Tactics for Changing Your Organization and the World by Ronald A. Heifetz, Marty Linsky, Alexander Grashow, published 2009.*
- *Reinventing the Organization: How Companies Can Deliver Radically Greater Value in Fast-Changing Markets by Arthur Yeung & Dave Ulrich, Sept 2019.*
- *Organizational Theory, Design and Change | Seventh Edition | By Pearson Paperback – 26 December 2017 by R Jones Gareth (Author), Matthew Mary (Author).*
- *Coaching: The Secret Code to Uncommon Leadership by Ruchira Chaudhary: An all-in-one Business Guide & Business Coaching Book |Business Book teaches about New Model Business, Penguin by Ruchira Chaudhary, Jan 2021*

- *Leadership Reformed: Why Leaders Need the Gospel to Change the World (Routledge Frontiers of Business Management) by Sen Sendjaya, Dec 2019*
- *Jack Welch on Leadership: Abridged from Jack Welch and the GE Way (The McGraw-Hill Books in Brief) by Robert Slater, Mar 2004*
- *A Handbook on Corporate Leadership | Condensed Guide for Corporate Directors & Senior Executives (New Release) by Institute of Directors India, Apr 2022*
- *Primal Leadership: Unleashing the Power of Emotional Intelligence by Daniel Goleman, Richard Boyatzis & Annie McKee, Aug 2013*
- *Leadership Strategy and Tactics: Field Manual by Jocko Willink, Jan 2020*
- *Leadership: Discover the Qualities of Leaders and How to Use Them in Your Own Life for Ultimate Success by Benjamin Smith, Dec 2016*
- *Lincoln On Leadership For Today: Abraham Lincoln's Approach to Twenty-First-Century Issues by Donald T. Phillips, Feb 2018*
- *The Leader's Companion: Insights on Leadership Through the Ages by J. Thomas Wren, Aug 1995*
- *The Edge of Leadership: A Leader's Handbook for Success by Brigette Tasha Hyacinth, Mar 2017*
- *The Leadership Crisis and the Free Market Cure: Why the Future of Business Depends on the Return to Life, Liberty, and the Pursuit of Happiness by John A. Allison, Dec 2014*
- *Leadership by Values: The Proverbial Cwtch of the Panglossian by Ramesh Subramanian, Aug 2020*
- *Leadership: Essential Selections on Power, Authority, and Influence by Barbara Kellerman, Sep 2010*

www.ingramcontent.com/pod-product-compliance
Ingram Content Group UK Ltd.
Pitfield, Milton Keynes, MK11 3LW, UK
UKHW040007200726
13854UKWH00001B/76

9 798888 698914